Secret Attachments

Exposing the Roots
Of Addictions and Compulsions

Peter Michaelson

Prospect
Books

Secret Attachments

Exposing the Roots Of Addictions & Compulsions

Library of Congress Catalog Card Number: 92:83750

Publisher's Cataloging in Publication Data

Peter Michaelson

Secret Attachments: Exposing the Roots of Addictions and Compulsions.

Bibliography: p

1. Substance abuse–Therapy. 2. Compulsive Behavior–Therapy. 3. Drug Abuse–Treatment. 4. Psychoanalysis. 5. Applied Psychology. 6. Personal Growth.

ISBN: 1-882631-26-9

Manufactured in the United States of America

First **Prospect Books** Edition August 1993
836 Anchor Rode Dr., Naples, FL 33940

To Gordon and Martha

Author's Note

The names and identifying details of the case histories in this book have been changed to protect confidentiality. Any resemblances to persons living or dead is purely coincidental. Anyone with a history of emotional disorders, or who feels emotionally unstable, or who is taking psychiatric medication, should not do the exercises in this book without first consulting a mental-health professional.

Table of Contents

Chapter 1

The Addict's Emotional Nature

Marie was thirty-two-years old and had addictions to alcohol, prescription drugs, and food. She had been in two intensive treatment programs and had spent years in on-going support groups. Despite these efforts toward recovery, she still suffered from depression, severe relationship difficulties, low self-esteem, feelings of despair and failure about her life, as well as her inability to recover fully from her addictive behaviors.

She went through lengthy periods maintaining her abstinence, then suddenly fell back into her addictive mode. "I feel like I'm on a roller-coaster ride," she explained. "When I'm in my addiction, I feel like I'm possessed, taken over. I have no control. I'm so frustrated. I've tried everything, and I still feel like there's no hope."

Much of the focus of Marie's treatment was aimed at getting her to abstain from her addictions. Little attention, however, was given to Marie's real problems: her passive, dependent attitude toward others and her life, her sense of shame and self-hatred, and her conviction that others saw her as sick, inadequate, and defective.

Marie had a history of disappointments in her personal and family relationships. Her belief that she would be hurt and betrayed in relationships caused her to avoid emotional involvements with others. She had been unable to establish a feeling of confidence in herself on which to base independent decisions, and she was meshed in feelings of powerlessness and ongoing expectations of failure. She responded to herself and the world like a child, regarding others around her as authority figures who knew what was best for her. Like a child, she believed she was unable to handle her life adequately on her own.

Even while abstinent, Marie felt deep resentment for her helpless dependence on others, and she subjected herself to constant self-reproach for her lack of personality and her appearance. She often succumbed to erratic, emotional outbursts, which were followed by withdrawal and depression. Her chronic moodiness evoked rejection and disapproval from others, leaving her feeling more inadequate. She often retreated into a world of daydreams and fantasy in which she frequently saw herself being victimized by family, friends, or circumstances.

Millions of others like Marie are struggling with addictive behaviors, and find themselves unable to curb their abuse of alcohol, drugs, tobacco, and food. Others are compulsive about work, sex, shopping, or gambling. Like Marie, many have succeeded at being abstinent for long periods, but continue to struggle with feelings of self-condemnation, passivity, failure, and the conviction they will be rejected and abandoned if they reveal their true selves.

The extent of addictive behaviors among the population is like the national debt—it's bad and getting worse. The addiction epidemic affects us all, from the family to the community to the strength of the nation. True, human nature has always had and acted out its dark side. But it may be that some new disharmony with nature and ourselves is placing a new strain on our emotional equilibrium.

Eating disorders such as bulimia and anorexia have spread like plagues in the last twenty years. Previously these conditions were relatively rare. Obesity is substantially worse now than two generations ago, especially among children. Compulsive gambling is recognized as a greater problem than ever. Alcoholism has proliferated, and treatment centers spring up to handle the crisis. Phobias are said to be a growing problem.

This era is greatly different from our grandparents' time. Back then, people did not have all the choices, leisure time, and abundance we have. Often education or travel was not an option; many had to work hard and struggle just to survive. Fewer people were likely to binge on food because it was not available in such variety and quantity. When people worked hard all day to put meat and potatoes on the table, they did not worry about how slim and sexy they looked.

When Americans struggled to eke out a living, there was a legitimate reason to suffer. They did not have to account for why they were unhappy. They were all in it together. It was not by choice. It was how it had to be. Now with all our leisure and materialism, there is no apparent reason to suffer. But we suffer nonetheless. It is more urgent now that we understand why, so we can act wisely and enjoy our new leisure and abundance.

Important questions need to be addressed before we can resolve this problem on an individual and national level. We need to understand the true origins of addictive behaviors and why they are so resistant to treatment. We need to know why the addict denies the seriousness of his problem, and why it is so hard for him to see the negative consequences of his behaviors for himself and others.

This book gives you *more* than answers to these questions.

It represents a breakthrough in the comprehension of addictions and compulsions and offers a new approach to addiction treatment. After years of working in clinical practice with hundreds of addictive personalities, I have concluded that addictive behaviors are the result of underlying emotional problems, all of which have their roots in childhood.

Once we access the roots of these emotional issues and connect the emotions with their origins in childhood, symptomatic addictive behaviors gradually cease.

To put it bluntly, addictive personalities have not grown up and matured emotionally. They have not developed a strong sense of self and remain mired in childlike, egocentric ways of relating to the world.

Certain psychological traits are consistent with the expression of addictive behaviors. These traits are defense mechanisms that mask an addict's unresolved emotional issues from childhood.

1) A typical addict denies the existence of a problem. "I just like the taste," he says of his increasing use of alcohol. "I've got it under control," he adds. "I can quit at any time." He cons himself into believing that he does not have a problem.

Denial serves the underlying wish to continue his or her self-defeating behavior. If the addict admits he has a problem, then he is expected to do something about it, to take responsibility for his behavior. Denial also allows the addict protection against seeing himself as emotionally unstable or inadequate. In his mind, seeing the truth about himself requires that he face his greatest fear–the shame and humiliation of seeing himself as he truly is.

2) The addict is self-absorbed and self-centered. He is obsessed with alleged hurts or grievances and convinced he is the victim of others who reject or hurt him or want to make him submit to their control.

He finds it hard to give to others or respond to their needs because, emotionally, he feels entitled to be stroked, validated, and supported (treated like a child). Because of his insatiable emotional needs, he is unable to consider the dire consequences of his behavior on himself and on others. He is focused totally on his own needs and does not see others for who they are, but only as players in *his* life. This egocentric perspective leaves him unable to feel empathy for others or to be open to their feelings or points of view.

3) The addict cannot take criticism or accurate evaluation of his personality and behavior. Criticism merely reinforces what he already unconsciously feels about himself—that he is wrong and worthless. Therefore, he blames others for all his problems and makes others responsible for his unhappiness. To avoid recognition of his own flaws and emotional issues, the addict reduces and criticizes others. He will put down or reject anyone who dares to insinuate that he has a problem. He will take any form of disagreement or attempt to get him to see his problem as betrayal. He is extremely defensive to any real or imagined slight.

His spouse's words and reactions are a mirror-image of his own inner conscience. Both hound him for his self-defeating behavior, producing unwanted guilt. What he really wants is to indulge in his behavior without that nagging guilt.

Often addicts are focused on self-blame and self-reproach. Internally, they berate themselves with statements such as: "I'm no damn good. I can't do anything right. I'm weak and stupid. There's no way I can lick this thing." Self-reproach only heightens suffering; it does nothing to get to the heart of the problem.

4) Like an adolescent, an addict often brags and presents a superior, know-it-all facade. He may embellish his accomplishments or verbally hold the floor as a way to seek attention and approval from others. Like a child, he wants the attention focused on him. He sees himself and his outlook as superior

and right. This behavior masks his attachment to being ignored and indicates an inner conviction that he is nothing special.

5) The addict has a hard time accepting help. Change is felt to be too much effort, involving too much deprivation, the giving up of something he considers pleasurable. In his mind, change also involves being pressured by some outside force that makes him do something he really does not want to do. He feels great resistance to the feeling that he is being required or forced to change. He has no qualms sabotaging the good in his life to establish in his mind how much he hates being controlled and told what to do.

Help or insight is also taken as an indication that he is wrong and bad. He experiences insight into his behavior as criticism and condemnation, and consequently he feels shamed and humiliated. That is why he finds it so hard to reveal himself to anyone or admit his mistakes.

6) The addict is terrified of giving up the substance or the behavior. Without it, he feels as if he will fall apart. Compulsive behaviors give him the feeling of keeping himself "intact." For some addicts, the substance is a substitute for a "self." The substance or the behavior is a crutch that provides him with a pseudo-feeling of confidence or well-being. The crutch keeps his psychological defenses in place (or his unresolved emotional issues at bay), at least temporarily. This is why he feels he has no choice but to choose his addiction over his loved ones. He feels he will fall apart without the addictive behavior.

7) The addict exhibits Dr. Jekyl and Mr. Hyde mood swings. At any moment, he can fly into a rage or depression over some insignificant injustice. This behavior mirrors the self-centeredness of a child. He is terrified of his inner feelings of despair, frustration, sadness, and vulnerability and uses the substances to keep these feelings suppressed. The addict is out of touch with his feelings in general and exhibits a limited emotional repertoire. Often anger is the only feeling he expresses. Most

addicts are filled with anger and rage.

An addict is prone to feelings of helplessness and self-pity. One minute he is a mighty tyrant raging at his loved ones, the next a whimpering child who feels powerless in controlling his life.

8) Addicts have a very difficult time communicating with others. Often they mask and hide their feelings. Unable to assert themselves in an appropriate adult manner, they lash out in anger. Honest communication carries the prospect of being found out as wrong, inadequate, and worthless. Any expression of "the real me" brings forth shame and humiliation.

9) The addict is an emotionally dependent person who refuses to admit to his dependency on others. His dependency on others is mirrored by his dependency on a substance or a compulsive behavior. Feeling powerless to control his life and his relationships with others, he becomes powerless to a substance that controls and runs his life.

10) An addict anticipates rejection and abandonment. Ironically, he brings about the rejection he fears the most with his *negative exhibitionistic behavior* (obnoxious, angry, rude, foolish, overweight) that drives people away.

If others should reject him, he makes them out to be the villain rather than examine his own behavior. He harps on the faults of others, creating the illusion that he is the victim of their abuse and betrayal. He has a profound attachment to being "an innocent victim of someone else's malice,"and conveniently rearranges reality to fit his victim perspective.

11) Like an adolescent, he engages in secretive behavior. He frequently lies to cover up his tracks and evade the influence of others. In his mind, he lies to protect himself so he won't be looked down upon as weak and bad. But, subconsciously, he is really setting himself up to be caught and punished like a naughty child. He is secretly attached to feelings of being shamed, controlled, and punished. Although he protests how

much he hates those feelings, he sets himself up to get more of what he says he hates. His lying, for instance, is soon discovered by others and repercussions follow.

12) In his self-destructiveness, he shows little or no concern or value for his health and well-being. He is steeped in self-hatred, and he projects that hatred onto others, seeing them as hateful or imagining that they hate him. His substantial negativity has a depressive effect on his vitality and his will to live and to thrive, and consequently he shows in his self-destructive behavior how little he values his life.

13) Many addicts can be superficially quite charming and charismatic. Charm is unconsciously cultivated as a way to distract attention away from the addict's negative behaviors, as well as a way to extract positive stroking and approval. Many addicts thrive on being able to outwit, outsmart, and outperform others, as part of their on-going attempts to prove their value and worth. In their egocentricity, they are preoccupied with their self-image and how they are seen by others. Image is more important to them than being real.

So what can people do to break free of these childish behaviors and put an end to all the suffering that accompanies addictive behaviors? The single most important element is *insight.* Addictive personalities have to understand themselves and their emotional reactions more fully. Otherwise, their recovery will be incomplete, marred by discontent and unhappiness.

The trick for an addictive personality is to see the immature and childish components in himself. This process involves penetrating his unconscious mind for insight into the meaning of his cravings, desires, motivations, beliefs, feelings, and behaviors. This book facilitates the acquisition of insight through exercises and techniques. As well, insight is provided by numerous case studies in which I delve into the hidden meaning and significance of addictive behaviors and the emotional attachments that accompany them.

This book is a road map explaining the origins and nature of addictive behavior, highlighting the secret attachments to negative feelings that plague addictive personalities, and providing escape routes from this prison of suffering. It is full of hope for those individuals who feel out of control, taken over by an inner agenda that leaves them floundering, and lost in some emotional wasteland.

Chapter 2

Roots of Addictive Behaviors

An addiction to a particular substance or to a behavior is a metaphor for the addict's deeper problem: *emotional addictions to certain negative states that are left-over or unresolved from childhood.*

Addictive or compulsive individuals are unconsciously addicted to unpleasant emotional experiences that fall into three categories.

The first category is deprivation. This means the individual focuses on, and indulges in, feelings of being deprived, denied, refused, drained, not getting, missing out, short-changed, ripped off, never satisfied, and loss.

Bill, a 42-year-old alcoholic, exemplified this problem. He felt his wife never gave him enough sex, even though they had sex almost daily. He believed she did not love him enough, support him enough, nor respond to him the way he wanted. His wife Sally felt drained and frustrated with his insatiable "neediness." Bill did not know it at the time, but he secretly wanted to feel that Sally was "refusing" him somehow or other. Sally usually went out of her way to try to satisfy him, but this did not really impress him because he was more involved emotionally in experiences of refusal. He was able to see and feel refusal even in situations where none was intended.

The second category of addictions involves feeling controlled, dominated, forced to go along with the agenda of others, and feeling helpless at the mercy of others or of forces beyond one's control. Addicts expect to be taken advantage of, trapped, and obligated. They are addicted to powerlessness, and that is evident in their feelings of being at the mercy of a substance or behavior.

Lilly, another alcoholic in her fifties, spent her twenty-five years of marriage passively dependent on her dominating husband. She let him make all the decisions and even allowed him to pick out her clothes and tell her what to wear. She felt she could not make a move without his permission. Her drinking was a manifestation of her unconscious willingness to be controlled, dominated and invalidated by any person, force, or substance she came under the influence of.

Finally, in the third category, some individuals are addicted to feelings of rejection, betrayal, criticism, feeling disapproved, being seen in a negative light, condemned, excluded, and abandoned. They are caught up in feelings of being caught, shamed, and punished.

James, a banker in his thirties, stayed out late drinking heavily at bars. To appease his wife, he made up stories about clients and the necessity of working in the evenings. He flirted with the prospect of getting caught in his lies, which happened regularly, and secretly he played on old feelings from childhood of getting caught and being shamed. In addition, he experienced his wife's cold withdrawal of affection and her threats of punishment, which had been major dynamics in his relationship with his mother.

The addictions to these feelings are unconscious, and so I refer to them as *secret attachments.* They are the result of unresolved childhood feelings and experiences with one's parents and siblings that are carried over and transferred onto people or circumstances in an addict's present life. It is the unconscious addiction to these old negative emotions that makes the addict behave so childishly and facilitates his self-defeating and self-destructive behaviors.

To put it another way, addictive personalities unconsciously recreate and recycle old childhood expectations of being deprived, denied, criticized, rejected, and forced to submit in the contexts of their present lives. Since they have not worked out these feelings, they have *secret attachments* to them which cause these individuals to become repeatedly entangled in experiences that produce these old feelings. To repeat, these unconscious attachments to feelings of deprival, refusal, control, criticism, rejection, and so on are like *emotional addictions.* Most addictive personalities are in complete denial of their emotional addictions (through the clever operation of their defense mechanisms).

These emotional addictions or secret attachments result in a childish, victim mentality that must be transformed before self-defeating reactions and behaviors are given up for good. It is this childish mentality that causes the anger, fear, sadness, frustration, envy, loneliness, and a host of other negative emotions that compel an addict to act out with addictive or compulsive behavior.

I am convinced no permanent transformations occur without the addict taking personal responsibility for his addictive behavior and the underlying emotional reactions and feelings that cause him to act out in self-defeating ways. It is true that an addict may be able to stop his addictive acting out without working through his underlying emotional problems, but he will usually resort to another form of addictive or compulsive behavior (shifting addictions) or remain mired in the same childish mentality that caused his addictive behavior and now causes ongoing anxiety, dissatisfaction, and unhappiness.

Abstinence, in my view, is not the final indicator of recovery or transformation. It is only the beginning. Unless we release repressed or unresolved negative emotions, we cannot possibly become self-aware and confident in a way that would preclude the chance of reverting under stress to our old self-defeating behaviors. Addicts need insight into why they feel the way they do in the minutes and hours before they succumb to their addictions and compulsions.

It may be emotionally challenging and difficult for many readers to accept and understand how we can become addicted to negative emotions because this process is unconscious and not experienced first-hand. It is hard to see deeply into ourselves because of our psychological defenses and resistance to facing unpleasant truths about ourselves.

Traditional treatment methods say that genes, biochemical imbalances, or "the disease of addiction" are responsible for our failures and limitations. The more we believe this, the more we remain stuck in a victim position, convinced that, "I am not passive and attached to failure and defeat. On the contrary, my problem is that I have a disease. It is the disease that controls me." This belief absolves an individual of personal responsibility.

Self-responsibility does have the effect of making us anxious. Our inner conscience may be taunting us with, "Look at you, you loser. This mess is really your fault. You don't really want to succeed." It is comforting to defend ourselves with words such as, "It's not my fault. It's those damn genes!"

Difficult as it seems, it is the acceptance of individual responsibility for our lives and the recognition of our unconscious attachments to negative feelings that set us free. My system of therapy teaches people that they can manage their lives, and that they are not at the mercy of powers beyond their control.

The system described in this book works because I show the addictive personality how to disengage from his childish, victim mentality. An addictive personality can transform himself by understanding emotionally, not just intellectually, the following principles:

(1) The addict understands that he does have a free will and is responsible for his life and his behavior. He must learn to take personal responsibility for his distressful life circumstances and his emotional reactions to others. He learns to abstain from blaming, rationalizing his behavior, or making other people responsible for his emotional reactions.

(2) The addict learns that taking responsibility means understanding his negative emotions and reactions, and that means defining the deeper feelings that prompt his negative reactions. In other words, why is he feeling angry? What does he believe the other person is doing to him? Where does this feeling come from? He learns to understand the origins of his fears and feelings. He learns why he continues to hold onto them. He asks himself why he is sad and depressed. Rather than repressing his feelings with platitudes, excuses, or magical gestures such as the alleged forgiveness of his "tormentors," he searches for the meaning of his emotions and takes responsibility for them.

(3) The addict learns that most of his present emotional reactions are based on unresolved childhood hurts and grievances with his parents and siblings that he unconsciously transfers onto his present relationships with others, in ways that convince him he is once again being victimized. He learns to correlate these current feelings with his past feelings from childhood and to recognize his unconscious willingness to continue to indulge in refusal, deprival, criticism, rejection, and passive submission to the control of others. His parents may indeed have been ignorant, abusive, or neglectful—but the

addict's problem in the present is his ongoing, unconscious willingness to continue being hurt by old feelings from his past.

(4) The addict understands that the child part of his psyche is controlling his emotional experiences, and that this inner-child part, despite its innocence and sweetness, is also self-centered, egocentric, and convinced that others do not have its best interests at heart. He learns how his inner child has misinterpreted and misunderstood his parents' intentions, beliefs, and actions. He sees how he continues to misinterpret the intentions of others and how he has incorporated his parents' self-defeating behavior and beliefs in his present life. He learns to recognize when he is in his child mode and learns to question why the child part of his psyche is reacting to present circumstances in such a self-defeating manner.

(5) The addict understands that he is not helpless or powerless over his addictive behavior once he learns how he transfers the past onto the present, once he learns to define his feelings towards himself and others, and once he gains insight into his self-defeating emotional reactions. His addictive behavior can be overcome, but that requires an emotional understanding of how he unconsciously provokes others into expressing negative feelings towards him and how he uses injustices or the weaknesses of others as opportunities to indulge in negative feelings. In this way, he learns how to become self-responsible rather than depending on external crutches to keep him from acting out addictively.

(6) Finally, the addict must want to change his self-defeating emotional reactions and develop the motivation and belief that he can transcend his addictive identity. He must believe that he can learn to have confidence in himself and his decisions, and lead a balanced and happy life without the fear of relapsing into his addictive behavior.

To demonstrate how this process of unconscious addiction to negative emotions persists from childhood into our adult lives, let us look at the following example.

Jane, a compulsive overeater in one of my weight-loss groups, had a secret attachment to being criticized and seen as inadequate. Once when I unexpectedly met Jane on the street, she said, "Oh, my hair is such a mess!" Another time she apologized for the clothes she was wearing, saying, "I just came from the gym." I had not noticed anything particular about her hair or her clothes. To me she looked fine.

But Jane believed that I (and others who saw her) observed her critically, that my eyes were spotlights looking for her flaws, and consequently she felt compelled to defend herself. This was the essence of her problem. Jane was steeped in the expectation of being criticized and seen as inadequate, dating back to how she felt as a child in her relationship with her father. She described her father as a perfectionist who found fault with everyone. He constantly picked at Jane and harped on her flaws and inadequacies. He never praised her or acknowledged her good points.

Her reaction to perceived criticism or disapproval in her adult life was to feel inadequate and subsequently to overeat. Then she began to criticize and disapprove of herself (acting like her father) for overeating and gaining weight, thereby intensifying her feelings of inadequacy. She would make herself feel worse as she imagined how other people were looking at her critically and rejecting her for her obesity.

Jane had recently gone through a prolonged and bitter divorce in which she was devastated by the criticism and blame leveled at her by her spouse, who had responded to her with the same kind of disapproval as her father.

Another time Jane went out of her way to praise me profusely, out of proportion to my actions. In order to defend against her unconscious attachment to criticism, she consciously strove to be praised and complimented and to give to others the praise and recognition that she said she wanted for herself. She flattered me because, from her perspective, the feeling of being praised must have been as important to me as it was to her.

Like every addictive personality, Jane was plagued by negative perceptions about herself and the world. She was quick to take things personally. She interpreted certain events and behaviors of others as being directed personally against her. She hung onto grudges and nursed the hurt and humiliation of alleged or real slights and mistreatment. She was a specialist in the art of misunderstanding events and the motives of others.

Unaware she possessed this self-centered mentality, she was convinced that her grudges, grievances, and dissatisfactions were legitimate, caused by the malice of others, the harshness of life, or her own failures and inadequacies. She did not understand that the problem was her own emotional propensity to personalize her reaction to people and events in her life.

On a conscious level, an addictive personality like Jane wants to prosper and be happy, but the unconscious child part remains inclined to look for experiences or opportunities to feel deprived, controlled, or rejected. These secret attachments to negative feelings are protected from our conscious awareness and kept in operation by the defense mechanisms of anger, blame, denial, excuses, and projection. For example, whenever Jane felt criticized, she protested and complained vigorously how much she hated it.

Jane challenged me on one occasion, "How can I be attached to criticism when I hate it so much."

"Your hating it is part of your defense," I replied. "Your angry or hateful reaction to criticism or perceived criticism distracts you from becoming aware of the degree to which you are secretly willing to indulge in feeling criticized. If this were not the case, there would be no need for you to react emotionally to being criticized–you would simply assess the criticism based on who it was coming from and for whatever value or truth it might contain and either ignore it or learn from it. But instead you suffer a painful emotional reaction. You become a victim of the one who criticizes or appears to criticize.

"This problem goes a step further," I added. "There may even be times when, unconsciously, you provoke criticism from others, meaning you collude secretly in the creation of events or circumstances that produce the feeling of being criticized. Then you react with righteous indignation when criticism happens. For example, take the problem of your weight. There is a secret pay-off for you in your overeating and weight gain: this behavior feeds your attachment to feeling criticized and rejected. You become very critical of yourself and condemn yourself for your lapses and binges. As well, you imagine others looking at you critically as you put on weight. This is how you act out your secret attachment to feeling criticized."

Secret attachments are emotional addictions that exist in the unconscious mind and cannot be scientifically evaluated under a microscope. Supported only by clinical evidence and theory, secret attachments have been misunderstood and overlooked. Nevertheless, they are real, and recognition of them needs to be incorporated into mental-health and addictive treatment programs to improve their effectiveness.

Chapter 3

Dancing With the Dark Side

That we all have a negative side of ourselves is readily apparent. The opposing human conditions of truth and falsehood, courage and cowardice, good and evil, have been expressed dramatically in mythology, religion, and literature since the dawn of humanity. Men and women cannot escape participation in the battle between these antagonistic forces. The struggle for the pre-eminence of the positive over the negative, for pleasure over pain, is the essence of the human drama.

The clash of the positive and the negative is illustrated in the world's greatest literature–the Greek tragedies, Shakespeare's plays, in the novels of Dickens, Dostoyevsky and Melville. Dante's *The Divine Comedy* portrays the "Inferno," a netherworld symbolic of the negative side. Dante's shadowy underworld is a place of suffering, and the allegory depicts an epic struggle between good and evil for the soul of man.

More recently, Luke Skywalker in the *Star Wars* series faces his inner demons who urge him to follow in the steps of his evil father Darth Vadar. "Come into the dark side of the force," the father begs his son. Luke must use all his inner resources to resist the seductive appeal of the dark side. Literature, myths, and legends tell us that true heroism is the adventure of self-discovery and the pursuit of liberation from an oppressive negative force.

Jill, in recovery from drug and alcohol abuse, revealed this human struggle when she said in a session, "I'm feeling a build-up of pressure. I'm being tempted to get back to drinking and drugging. You know what it is—I want to be bad. I can really feel how much I want to be bad. It's fun and exciting and hard to resist."

Jill had felt shamed, criticized, and disapproved of during her childhood, and through that experience she had acquired a secret unconscious attachment to those feelings. As an adult, she saw others as criticizing her and disapproving of her, and unconsciously she indulged in these negative feelings. In fact, her impulse to drink and to take drugs was caused in part by her conviction that she was a bad person. Consciously, however, she was only aware of her suffering—her fear of relapsing and the waves of self-reproach and self-condemnation that washed over her whenever she acted out with her addictive behavior. She gave herself the condemnation she was unconsciously looking for from others.

The dark side of our nature is symbolically represented as the dragon's liar in the legends of brave knights and beautiful damsels, in the tragic undercurrents of the *Iliad* and the *Odyssey,* in the tales of Siegfried and St. George. Ancient heroes and heroines liberated themselves from sinister villains and evil forces in their savage world. The archetypal image of a devil is based on the intuitive awareness of a sinister power entirely opposed to our well-being. The devil represents a power that not only initiates human suffering but also takes great satisfaction in it. Individuals tend to project the devil image outward upon real or imagined entities. This is a defense mechanism: the more someone sees the devil in others, the more he will feel pure and innocent and blind to his own dark side. Unfortunately, the more easily he also will hate others and make enemies out of mere shadows.

Where do secret attachments to negative emotions fit in this struggle between the negative and the positive? Metaphorically, secret attachments to negative emotions are like black holes of outer space. Black holes cannot be seen directly and no light escapes from them because of their extreme gravity. In a comparable way, very little light shines on secret attachments because they are in the unconscious mind behind a heavy curtain of psychological defenses. Black holes are detected by their gravitational influence on other bodies or energy systems in their vicinity. Secret attachments are detected and understood through our patterns of self-defeat, our misery, substance abuse, compulsive behavior, obsessions, phobias, and by our negative impact on others.

The addictive personality is pulled into the negative vortex within himself. Like mass in a black hole, he becomes rigid, closed, contracting, trapped in an inner darkness that makes him feel powerless. The addictive personality is aware only of the outer manifestations of his secret attachments which include stress, dissatisfaction, boredom, worry, fear, guilt, anger, hurt, anxiety, confusion, loneliness, dissension, depression, shame, self-absorption, and so on.

In part, the existence and significance of secret attachments have not been appreciated because modern psychology has demoted the unconscious as a source of insight. Even before Sigmund Freud's death in 1939, psychology had begun to splinter into numerous competing theories and treatment procedures. Mental-health professionals exhibited a tendency to promote their own interpretations. Practitioners began to shift from the Freudian focus on the unconscious, as new frontiers of inquiry opened in social psychology, family systems theory, cognitive approaches, behaviorism, gestalt, and humanistic and transpersonal psychology. Little consensus now exists on the tenets or principles of psychology.

Nowadays it is fashionable to resort to the use of medical drugs to alleviate symptoms of emotional disorders. This means that emotional problems are made out to be medical problems. I believe that the use of pharmaceuticals does have its place and is appropriate and useful in severe emotional disturbances and cases of acute depression and phobias. But use of pharmaceuticals does not represent a cure. Drugs merely alleviate symptoms, allowing patients to be "managed." Drugs cannot cure or transform an underlying self-defeating mentality.

Modern psychiatry promotes a "pill-popping" culture in the mistaken belief that internal chemical adjustments will cure mental and emotional disorders, and alleviate self-defeating and self-destructive behavior. Without accompanying psychotherapy, drugs cannot resolve unconscious conflicts. People become smarter, wiser, and more discerning when they work out their unconscious emotional problems with the help of a therapist and a support group.

The promotion of psycho-pharmacology is, in my view, also suspect because of the potential for huge and easy profits. The most profitable corporations in the world are drug companies. And many psychiatrists have failed to develop psychotherapeutic skills because of their reliance on prescribing drugs.

The public's widespread use of sedatives and anti-depressants raises the specter of "authority-validated drug dependency," a situation of great appeal to some addictive personalities because it condones their attachment to passivity and their willingness to depend on a substance to get them through life. The medical and pharmaceutical industries are claiming that certain behaviors are "beyond our control." This philosophy is being promoted with billions of dollars of advertising, and could cause us eventually to lose control of ourselves and our world. To insist that addictions are caused by "bad" genes, or biochemical imbalances, or a "disease" is a form of denial and repression that absolves the individual of personal responsibility for his emotional reactions and self-destructive behaviors. Some addictions authorities have even proposed that shoplifting is a "disease." What next? Criminal acts?

Modern psychology's use of drugs or superficial behavioristic therapies that detour around the unconscious are due in part to the extreme difficulty in scientifically studying the unconscious. The unconscious can not be quantified, measured, or seen under a microscope. It is delineated only by theory and the weight of circumstantial evidence. Psychology, under pressure to be scientific and to produce "hard facts," turned to the study of human and animal *behavior* where statistics and scientific analyses could be applied.

A large area of psychology began to develop an emphasis on the study of behavior–how individuals and groups respond to environmental stimuli–and ignored the unconscious. Once the unconscious was demoted, culture and environment became the perceived primary influences on the behavior of individuals. Neurosis and addictions were considered a consequence of inappropriate influences in the environment and in culture.

However, environment and culture are unintelligible without the participation of one's unconscious. It is usually not an event or situation in itself that poses an emotional problem, but how a person responds to it. For instance, one person accepts hard times as a challenge while another experiences it as a disaster.

Jean Piaget, the renowned childhood development researcher, discovered that what adults teach a child is not necessarily what the child learns. The child takes what is taught and reformulates it, redesigns it, based on his view of the world, in a process of assimilation and accommodation. Two children raised in the same family will experience relatively similar cultural and environmental influences. Yet they often turn out to be entirely different in their temperament, in their personalities, in their prospects for success and happiness.

Authorities on addictive and compulsive behaviors suggest that the negative influences of parents are responsible for creating addictive personalities. Recovery-program leaders tell participants that a child is a sweet innocent who is corrupted by various forms of parental abuse and ignorance, resulting in low self-esteem and self-hatred. Negative influences, they say, include parental domination, undue exercise of power and control, repression of feelings, and violations of a child's sense of self.

Parents certainly do have a major influence on the future emotional health of a child. But the problem is more complicated than some addiction specialists realize. These specialists base their theories of infant and child development on subjective, sentimental projections of their own childhood desires for unconditional love, rather than exploring and understanding objective research on infant and child perceptions and behaviors.

The belief that parents are to blame for the addictive and compulsive behaviors of their children overlooks basic research supported by such notables as Sigmund Freud, Melanie Klein, Edmund Bergler, and Jean Piaget. Each child, because of the self-centeredness he is born with, comes into the world predisposed to *misinterpret the actions and intentions of the parents.* Each child is encumbered by the negative impact of his parents' weaknesses *and* the subjective manner in which he interprets the actions and attitudes of his parents toward himself. In other words, infants and children personalize their experiences with their parents and siblings, misinterpret them, and tend to perceive that parents and siblings are against them in some manner. Childhood perceptions and emotions linger on to create emotional difficulties later in life.

Our present emotional reactions are the result of an interaction between our parents' influence on our upbringing and our own personal way of interpreting how we were treated. I have observed that many addictive personalities have had good conventional upbringings. Moreover, many adults who have been raised in dysfunctional families have no addictive problems and manage their lives successfully.

Jean Piaget reported that children, because of their egocentrism and the illusion of being all-powerful, are unable to understand another person's point of view. This makes them essentially self-centered and selfish. Most normal children would like to get 100 percent attention on demand from their parents. They often feel that they do not get enough, and they focus on what they do not have, not on what they are given.

Children do not respond well to orders or chores and resist doing what you tell them to do. They do not take well to the word "No." They feel gypped, cheated, and unfairly treated with respect to other siblings. They can become jealous and easily feel excluded. They feel that whatever happens, they somehow caused it and feel responsible for just about everything. If a parent is upset, they are convinced it is because of their badness. As one parent described her two-year-old daughter, "She's like a demanding tyrant. I have to give her my total attention and give her what she wants or she'll go into a rage. No matter what I give her, she's never satisfied. I'm going nuts."

I remember the anxious and resentful feeling I had as a child that my sisters might get a bigger piece of dessert than me. At the table I watched intently to make sure they did not get more. As an adult, I noticed how this tendency to compare and feel unfairly given to had permeated my life. This emotional problem had nothing to do with my parents. It was the result of a childish reaction to perceiving the world as unfair towards me. I have heard the anguish of hundreds of parents who are at a loss to explain their children's convictions of unfair treatment when these parents have gone out of their way to be fair with each child.

Even when parents were controlling or abusive, continuing animosity toward them (which can be repressed and unconscious) indicates the adult son or daughter is holding them responsible for his or her problems. In other words, the child, and later on the adult, continues to choose to hold onto feelings of hurt and insult. He is willing to be affected and recreate the same familiar feelings long after parenting stops. For example, consider an alcoholic who says angrily, "I wouldn't be an alcoholic if my father had not been an alcoholic!" Even if this statement were true, the son's blaming attitude makes him feel less responsible for his own negative attitudes and behavior, and more prone to continue his self-damaging behavior.

He will use blame as a defense in other areas of his life to avoid seeing and being responsible for his own self-damaging tendencies. He will hold grudges against significant others in his life for the same problems he had with his father–feeling let down, a burden, unloved, and neglected. If he blames his parents, he is compelled to see significant others as pseudoparents (transference) who he feels are also against him in some way. As long as he holds grudges against his father, he holds onto his secret attachments to feeling disappointed and unloved, and he unconsciously remains determined to be the victim of his father.

This does not mean that, in order to be healthy, a son or daughter has to admire or love parents who may have been negligent or cruel. Cases of incest or physical abuse, for instance, can negate all claims on love. For the person's sake, however, *continuing to hold the parents responsible for his present-*

day problems will not serve a healthy purpose.

One of the major components of neurosis is the belief that we are innocent victims of the malice or neglect of others. This belief absolves the individual of personal responsibility for his external circumstances and for his emotional reactions.

Piaget's findings help us understand why humanity has resisted the notion of secret attachments. We make choices in what to believe, independent of reality. People cling to certain beliefs for emotional reasons. In the Middle Ages people hated being told the scientific findings that the earth is not at the center of the universe. Because of their lingering infantile self-centeredness, people wanted to believe they were at the center. If the earth were not at the center, they felt insignificant, demoted in God's eyes. This feeling of being humbled is abrasive to the individual's sense of self-importance and narcissism. Millions of people also rejected Darwin's discovery in the 19th century that humanity was an evolution of the animal kingdom. They rejected him because he took away their feelings of being special, no longer personally favored by God, not created in His image. People also cling to certain beliefs on the narcissistic presumption that everything worth knowing about human nature is already known.

People see what they want to see, they hear what they want to hear. Adults watching TV news will have profoundly different mental and emotional reactions to the same event. If some event does not fit in with their preconceived belief structure, it will be discounted. Emotionally, some people were not able to accept that the Holocaust took place. Others have refused to believe that men have landed on the moon.

Reality is filtered by our emotional investment in ego-preservation, or protection of narcissism. We have seen the emotional reactions to Copernicus, Darwin, and Freud who challenged our infantile self-centeredness. Adults remain "ego-centered" (egocentric) because of lingering infantile megalomania, the last holdout of the infant's conviction of its omnipotence. People want the sense that they are at the center, in charge, in control, and know what is going on in their lives. To recognize our secret attachments, however, is to come to an inner realization that is both humbling and frightening, for such recognition requires that we come face-to-face with an alien and self-defeating force within ourselves. As it turns out, the more we see into this side of ourselves, the more we gain in strength and self-control.

As a group, addictive personalities represent a cross-section of the population who are in a more critical showdown with this alien side of their human nature.

Freud believed in a self-destructive element in the psyche. He called it the *death drive,* and wrote that it constituted a force of self-aggression directed at the inner person from what he called the *superego.* Freud's final thoughts on the death drive were published posthumously in *An Outline of Psychoanalysis.* In this text, the role of the pleasure principle and the death drive were presented as the cornerstone of his understanding of mental health. However, his followers were loath to accept this view, and they declined to incorporate it into mainstream psychoanalysis. There were inferences that a decline in Freud's intellectual powers as he approached his death had contributed to this "alien" intrusion into his psychological framework. Very few psychologists and psychotherapists incorporate into their clinical practice the understanding of such an alien force at work undermining the conscious hopes and aspirations of their patients.

The death drive does not mean that people secretly want to kill themselves. Rather, it refers to self-aggression or self-hatred, and our tendency to put ourselves in situations that oppose our well-being. The death drive opposes our mental, emotional, and spiritual evolution. It is personified in the self-destructive addict who starves himself emotionally, who denies himself pleasure and joy, who endangers his health while being held back and poisoned by his own negative impressions and self-absorption.

A theory of the origins of secret attachments, backed by clinical evidence, was reported by Dr. Edmund Bergler (1900-1962) beginning in the 1940s. This Austrian psychiatrist received his medical degree from the University of Vienna in 1926 and later practiced in New York City for more than twenty years. Picking up where Freud left off, Bergler developed an explanation that accounts for much of humanity's emotional suffering and self-defeating behaviors. A primary problem is the development in children by the age of two of a repository of self-aggression (the super-ego) that becomes the main instigator of negative feelings. (The formation of this self-aggression is explained in Chapter 6 and Chapter 12.)

Bergler wrote twenty-two books and 275 articles published in professional journals describing ways that negative emotions are created, reinforced, and maintained. When he saw the resistance to his ideas, he offered an explanation in *Principles of Self-Damage,* published in 1958. He related a conversation with Dr. Ludwig Jekels in 1954. Jekels, 87 at the time, was a respected figure among Freud's old guard, as well as a collaborator with Bergler in the 1930s on several psychoanalytic papers.

Bergler asked Jekels why so many psychologists had failed to uncover the central importance of subconscious attachments to the negative. Jekels' answer was succinct: "The fourth narcissistic hurt." Jekels was alluding to Freud's famous statement that humanity has suffered three narcissistic mortifications: Copernicus's proof that the Earth is not the center of the universe, Darwin's discovery that humankind has evolved from lower animals, and Freud's revelation that man is not master in his own house but subject to subconscious irrational forces. The fourth hurt, Jekels said, is the realization of the extent of humanity's secret attachments to the negative side.

To recognize this "fourth hurt" feels like blasphemy. That recalls George Bernard Shaw's words, "All great truths begin as blasphemies."

Try this as an exercise. Go through your day and observe how often you find yourself worried or caught up in negative expectations about others and how they will respond to you. Watch how you personalize the behavior of others. Keep an eye on your critical inner voices that put you down and discount your abilities.

Taking emotional responsibility means understanding how you maintain your dissatisfactions about yourself and life. You need to see how attached you are to this negative perspective, which means seeing how tempted you are to indulge in negative feelings. This insight brings about a shift in your perspective, resulting in better feelings about life and about yourself.

Chapter 4

Nancy and Harold

To help readers understand more about the role of secret attachments, I introduce Nancy and Harold, two individuals who, in sessions with me, journeyed into the underworld of their psyches. Both left far behind them old entanglements in out-of-control addictions and compulsions.

Nancy and Harold not only freed themselves from addictive behaviors, but they achieved fundamental positive transformation. This analysis of their personalities and behaviors reveals how secret attachments were at the roots of their self-destructive tendencies.

Nancy grew up in a small southern town and used alcohol and marijuana to deal with emotional problems even before she left high school. Her father died of cancer when she was an adolescent, and she and her two sisters and brother were raised by her mother.

Almost every month when the family drove into the city, they would buy a new set of dishes. Nancy's mother released her frequent frustration and anger by hurling dishes against a wall. One night Nancy came home and found a barbecue fork stuck in that kitchen wall where her mother had thrown it. A sister had drawn a comic face around the fork and underneath had written *Nancy.*

She liked to make her mother angry, Nancy said. "But then I wouldn't face it. I would go out and go drinking, come back late and she would be madder than ever."

The summer before her senior year in high school, Nancy was at a party. She was making love to a boy in one of the bedrooms when a girlfriend walked in and flew into a rage. When school started in the fall, the girlfriend told other senior students that they were either her friend or they were Nancy's—they couldn't be friends to both. Nancy went through the year with hardly anyone at school speaking to her. She was hurt and humiliated and used alcohol, ate too much, and smoked marijuana to cope emotionally.

"Even when I was a little kid," Nancy remembered, "I did not want to be like my mother. I decided I wasn't going to get married and have kids." Her mother became "almost crazy" during her angry outbursts, "like she was having an epileptic fit," Nancy explained. "I decided anger was bad because it made mother crazy. My mother couldn't be reasoned with, or talked to. We just had to wait out her fits of anger."

I told Nancy, "You passively accepted and endured the hurt of your mother's outbursts, just as you passively accepted being scorned and rejected by your schoolmates. Then you masked your underlying feelings of rejection by acting out with alcohol, marijuana, and food. Substance abuse became your means of coping, but also your means of covering up your attachments to feelings of neglect and rejection."

Nancy was thirty-three years old when she began psychotherapy. She had been abstaining from alcohol for two years with the help of the Alcoholics Anonymous program. She had stopped bingeing on food and purging (throwing up) six months earlier following her involvement in a food-addiction program. Now she was ready to begin work on the roots of her addictive personality. She wanted to transform herself from an anxious woman who might relapse at any time to a confident person who would leave her life of addictions far behind.

Nancy had stopped the substance abuse but still suffered emotionally. Unconsciously, she was attached to feeling rejected and criticized by others. These were feelings she had experienced in the extreme in her relationship with her mother and during her senior year in high school.

She revealed some of these secret attachments when she told me about an incident in her adult life that caused her great discomfort. She was at a dance, and she told her dance partner that she and her husband were going sailing in the nude. The dance partner, it seemed to her, reacted with a strange silence and an expression of wry amusement. Nancy immediately felt anxious and regretted having told him about the sailing trip. In that moment she began to imagine that this man was imagining her naked and not liking what he saw. She felt rejected and inadequate, and later she became depressed and stayed that way for several days, not aware she was indulging in feelings of being rejected and inadequate.

Her partner on the dance floor may only have been reacting to her disclosure with his own awkward embarrassment, or perhaps he was considering how much he would like to be along on the trip. Nancy, however, interpreted his reaction through her own emotional perspective, according to her own secret attachments. She was also predisposed to blurt out potentially embarrassing revelations or to behave in inappropriate ways that would then trigger in her those old feelings from her past of being rejected and inadequate.

In one therapy session Nancy said, "I felt so depressed when my sister had her baby boy. When I spoke to her on the phone, I told her I wished it had been a girl. I don't even know why I said that." Nancy had no children herself, based on an agreement between herself and her husband. Nevertheless, the moment she heard of her sister's baby, she seized on the opportunity to feel deprived. Her depression was the result of her indulgence in "peeping" at what her sister got–a baby–and feeling deprived herself.

I told her, "A person normally feels pleasure in having a new nephew to enrich her life, and she enjoys watching him grow up. But an individual attached to deprivation finds some way to nullify the feeling of getting something good. It's like seeing the glass half empty instead of half full; your secret attachment to deprivation causes you to focus on what you are missing out on, rather than on what you are getting. The birth of a nephew becomes an opportunity for you to feel that something is now missing in your own life."

Nancy's depression after learning she had a new nephew was both a consequence of her secret attachment and a defense to cover it up. The defense goes like this, "How can you accuse me of being attached to feeling deprived! Look at how depressed I am! That's proof I don't want to be deprived." Nancy also defended against her attachment to feeling deprived when she told her sister of her preference for a girl–in order to play down the value of her sister's baby boy.

The following day someone brought a plateful of donuts into Nancy's office. With effort, she refrained from eating any. But twenty minutes later, responding to a sudden inner urge to be a mother, she was on the telephone to her health-insurance company inquiring about maternity-leave benefits. She was reacting again to a feeling of deprivation, triggered this time by the donuts as well as the news of her sister's baby. The reaction was another defense to cover up her attachment to being deprived: "You see, I'm not attached to missing out, I really would like to have a baby."

Nancy was on a food plan that restricted her diet. On a

visit home for Christmas, she sensed her secret willingness to indulge in feeling deprived of all the holiday treats and goodies her mother had prepared. She also felt deprived by what she considered the inexpensive and inappropriate presents her sisters gave her. Despite the temptations, she refrained from bingeing with food or reacting negatively toward her sisters.

Several days after her Christmas visit, she was returning some cosmetics to a department store when, as she perceived it, the clerk treated her rudely. Flushed and upset, Nancy went straight to the clothes department where, standing in front of a mirror holding a blouse, she berated herself for being fat and ugly.

This was another defense: rather than seeing that she was indulging in feeling rejected by the clerk, Nancy blamed herself for causing the incident, believing that "people treat me badly because I'm so fat and ugly." Once she accepted this defense, she felt even worse about herself, for she now had to contend with the self-reproach for allegedly being "fat and ugly."

"You took the treatment from the clerk personally," I said. "The clerk might have been in a bad mood for his own private reasons and been tempted to bark at anyone. But even if the clerk had been excessively rude, a healthy person would not be unduly agitated and would be able to let go of any unpleasant feelings within a few minutes. It's simply not appropriate to get caught up in the feeling of being the victim of some stranger's nasty disposition. But it happened because you seized upon the opportunity to indulge your secret attachments in feeling rejected."

Nancy continued her story. Back at the department store she found herself in the check-out line where, after waiting five anxious minutes with her credit card, she was again "rejected and refused" by another clerk because she was in the cash-only line. Somehow she had failed to see the cash-only sign (not surprising, since failure to see it served her secret willingness to become even more entangled in feelings of rejection and refusal). Before getting into the correct line, she bought a box of chocolates and that night began to binge. She felt a powerful impulse to give to herself (the chocolates) in order to cope with and cover up her attachment to feeling refused and rejected. However, in the predictable manner of self-defeating behavior, she binged emotionally on self-rejection for forty-eight hours after eating the chocolates.

When an individual slips into secret indulgence in some attachment such as rejection or refusal, self-defeating behavior is the likely consequence. Sometimes a series of triggering situations or events occur in close proximity, and the impulse to indulge the secret attachments becomes more than some individuals can resist.

Nancy was already harboring attachments to feeling denied and refused from the Christmas visit home. She was just barely managing to maintain her emotional equilibrium. When the opportunity to feel rejected and refused presented itself in the department store, she slipped over the edge of self-restraint. She was now primed for a full-blown relapse. As she binged, her feelings of rejection and disapproval intensified, becoming self-rejection and self-loathing as punishment for her relapse. "I beat up on myself all week," she groaned.

Nancy's food binge was an external rendition of her inner binge on rejection, refusal, and deprivation. Within a few days, and following a session in which her attachments were revealed and understood, Nancy was again feeling better about herself and in control of her eating habits. Since this event, her lapses have become few and far between, while her self-assurance and her capacity to enjoy her life have steadily increased.

Harold, a businessman in his forties, came to therapy distressed over his chronic ill humor and his inability to moderate his consumption of alcohol and food. He was plagued by doubt and recrimination and experienced powerful feelings of worthlessness.

One of two sons, Harold had been raised by a cranky dominating mother, an aloof father, and a grandmother who hated men. He endured, he said, savage beatings from his father. His father, however, only carried out these beatings at the insistence of Harold's mother. Harold's verbal battles with his mother were legendary, and on several occasions he was taken away in handcuffs by policemen called to his home by his mother after verbal altercations between them.

"My mother scared the hell out of me," Harold said. "I felt so inferior, and (as a result) I got no place with girls."

In school he did poorly. "I had no confidence," he remembered. "I played the class clown. I just felt bad as a person. My parents and teachers implied I was stupid." As an adult, he became compulsively critical and judgmental of others, just as his parents had treated him. (This behavior was a psychological defense against his own secret attachment to feelings of being inadequate, bad, and worthless.) It not only cost him peace of mind and friends but also business with certain customers he was quick to dislike.

Harold had dropped out of school at age sixteen, and before he turned twenty had become a voyeur and exhibitionist, prowling around at night either as a peeping Tom or in order to expose himself. His exhibitionism represented an acting out of his secret attachment to being seen in a negative light. As Harold exposed himself, he revived the familiar perception of being seen negatively by parents, teachers, and peers. There was a claim to power in this aspect of his unconscious defense: "I am not passively attached to being seen in a negative light. I am in charge, I am aggressive, I make it happen with my naughty behavior."

His voyeurism was another variation on his defenses, based on this rationale: "I'm not attached to being seen in a negative light. Look, on the contrary, I'm the one who goes out and sees others and tries to catch them doing bad things." Through his voyeurism, he identified with the people he "caught in the act" of doing something "bad," and in this way he indirectly revived his attachment to being seen critically.

"I have tremendous fear of women," Harold once said, "and see them as having a lot of power and authority over me." The guilty feelings produced by his exhibitionism made him feel dreadful about himself. He found comfort in his association with fundamentalist Christians who imposed a new control over him, one which in a supportive way helped him cope with the misery produced by his unconscious attachments. For a time, he considered becoming a minister.

Using prayer and willpower, he managed to get set up in business, and that "really helped me keep a grip on things," he said. When he came for therapy, he was married with two children. He had few friends. "I keep feeling people will find out I'm worthless and no good," Harold admitted. His only recreational activity was body-building, which he did compulsively. He realized from therapy that this activity was a compensation for inner feelings of worthlessness and an attempt to "prove" he wanted to be seen in a positive light (big muscles).

Harold also had a foot fetish. On the beach, he would be more attracted to a woman's feet than any other part of her body. In fantasies, he would see himself groveling at a woman's feet and feeling sexual delight in the act. He revealed that, when he was a youngster, his mother almost every evening sat in her comfortable lounge chair in the living room and put her bare and smelly feet up on a foot rest. From this position, she dominated the room, making her husband answer to her every whim.

"This foot fetish serves an unconscious purpose," I told

him. "One of your secret attachments is to the feeling of being controlled. The foot fetish allows you to embrace the feeling of being overpowered, dominated, and controlled by a woman, literally subjugated emotionally at the foot of the female. Your mother's feet perched regally upon the ottoman served as an early symbol of this female domination. Notice that you have continued to feel anxious and uncertain around strong, confident women."

When he was well into his thirties Harold remained an habitual marijuana user, and he only managed to give up marijuana by substituting alcohol and overindulgence with food. Despite sensations of ill health and warnings from his doctor about the strain on his heart, he had been unable to moderate this behavior.

He typically drank and overate in the evening while watching television. He would slip into a stupor, watching programming that he knew and felt to be boring, but which he nonetheless passively absorbed. When Harold ate and drank excessively in front of the TV set, he really got a double dose of control. He was not only possessed by the alcohol, but also by the TV set. His stupor was the acting out of his attachments to helplessness and powerlessness.

Whether he was giving in to the feeling of being taken over by his mother's dominating presence or by alcohol and TV, made no difference to his unconscious. All that mattered was his willingness to succumb to the feeling of being overcome, helpless, drained of his vitality, and powerless to alter his circumstances.

In one session, Harold expressed his great fear of having to stand up at a service-club luncheon, introduce himself, and say a few words about his business. The fear served as an unconscious defense: "But I do really want to be accepted–look at how nervous and fearful I am that I will not do well." Secretly, he was willing to indulge in feelings of being judged harshly and critically.

Harold was paranoid at times. For no apparent reason, he felt that his neighbors disliked him. When he realized this problem stemmed from his attachment to the feeling of being seen as inadequate or bad, the paranoia subsided.

When Harold was served with a subpoena to appear in small-claims court over a dispute with another businessman, he went home that night and "had seventeen or eighteen shots" of alcohol. "The adrenaline was really flowing and I couldn't even get drunk," he said. His primary emotion was fear of being caught at wrong-doing and exposed in the courtroom. Without being aware, he was "peeping," misusing his imagination, and seeing himself caught, shamed, and humiliated.

He claimed to have acted properly in this dispute, but whether or not he was innocent was incidental to his unconscious. His secret attachment to the feeling of being caught doing something bad or being exposed had intruded again into his life and was succeeding in taking over his emotional side. Guilty or innocent, this weakness would make it likely he would face the judge in court and, in his nervousness, behave as if he were guilty. In fact, this is what happened. Although he had good evidence on his side, his facial expressions, tone of voice, and body language exuded a guilty demeanor, and the judge found against him.

"Others do not make you feel a certain way," I told Harold. "When you reacted emotionally and began to drink heavily, you had already chosen to become entangled in feelings of being looked down upon as bad, although the choice was made unconsciously. Don't focus so much on the actions or motivations of the businessman who opposed you. Notice how you want to focus on the alleged injustice done to you by the other person, rather than to understand why you yourself are reacting so painfully to the situation. See how you yourself use this situation to indulge in feelings of being caught, shamed, and humiliated. You need to become aware of your willingness to use this situation to indulge in those feelings. The more you become aware of that, and see those attachments operating in other aspects of your life, the more your attachments will go away."

Several years earlier, an IRS audit of Harold's business had caused him to go through months of nervous anguish. In the end, he paid a few thousand dollars more in taxes but was absolved of any intentional wrongdoing. Again, his guilt or innocence was not the issue: he had seized on the opportunity to indulge in feeling caught, shamed, and condemned, which caused him unnecessary suffering.

By drinking excessively in reaction to the subpoena, Harold piled one addiction on top of another. On the top layer was his addiction to the alcohol. The bottom layer was his secret attachment (a kind of emotional addiction) to the feelings of being exposed, caught, or condemned. The alcohol abuse was a symptom of the attachments to these feelings. Liquor was used to tranquilize his inner turmoil but it soon became a crutch that crippled him more. This courtroom episode became an emotional repetition of the exhibitionism of his younger years when he had been exposing himself sexually to others and flirting with the prospect of being caught.

Both Harold and Nancy were tangled in secret attachments to feelings of being refused, controlled, dominated, rejected, and betrayed. Until they worked out these attachments in therapy, they had stumbled over them everywhere they turned. But most treatment programs ignore secret attachments, and thereby do not give people deep enough understandings of the nature and origins of their self-defeating impulses. Without that insight, an individual's self-awareness is too shallow to challenge the powerful self-defeating tendencies that are the product of secret attachments.

For example, Nancy ate the chocolates because of a strong impulse to give to herself in compensation for her indulgence in feeling rejected and refused by the store clerks. She unconsciously looked for opportunities to interpret rejection and refusal in the actions of people around her. Her resulting emotional reaction made it extremely tempting–if not irresistible–for her to resort to her familiar mode of self-defeating behavior and to binge on food.

A behaviorist would say to Nancy such things as (1) she did not use sufficient will power to resist buying the chocolates, (2) she made a poor choice out of the options available to her, (3) she did not employ positive affirmations to counteract the impulse to buy the chocolates, and (4) she ought to have avoided a location where temptation might arise. These recommendations are more like advice than insight. Advice is often cheap; insight is always precious.

I had Nancy observe and keep track in a journal of daily occurrences where she experienced rejection and refusal. The focus was not on whether others actually did reject or refuse her–*but on her seeing and understanding her own propensity to interpret a situation as rejection and refusal, and then to indulge unconsciously (and often consciously) in those feelings.*

Once she became entangled in the feelings of rejection and refusal, she could not avoid powerful emotional reactions such as anger, anxiety, depression, fear, worry, shame, and so on. This emotional distress was then manifested for all to see in behaviors that were self-defeating and self-destructive.

As Nancy began to understand her attachments to feeling rejected and refused, she no longer jumped at the opportunity to seek out feelings of refusal and rejection. She came to understand that rude treatment from another person may have nothing to do with her, but that it was probably an indicator of the mentality or attitude of the other person. Nancy weaned herself of her interest in being an emotional victim of another person's bad attitude. Consequently, her impulse to buy chocolates and other binge foods was greatly diminished.

Some people have said that looking at the negative side of ourselves reinforces the negative at the expense of the positive. They want to ignore the negative and concentrate solely on the positive. This is a slick form of denial and repression. The more that the negative side is seen and exposed, the more room there is for a "permanent positive" to exist. I delve into the negative side in order to help my clients become liberated from it. The addictive personality will not get far with positive affirmations and wishful thinking. Clean bandages over dirty wounds do not produce genuine healing.

Chapter 5

Hidden Feelings

A person's discovery of his secret attachments is a discovery of repressed or hidden feelings.

Ralph came for psychotherapy at his wife's insistence. She was concerned about his alcohol consumption and about the deterioration of his relationship with his teenage son. The wife complained of Ralph's rigid mentality and what she called his no-fun approach to life.

Ralph's son felt his father was excessively stern and restrictive. Ralph would become angry at his wife for allegedly undermining his authority whenever she gave in to their son's requests. When Ralph was a boy, he endured his father's strong willed, very strict approach to raising children. He claimed that the whippings and beatings he received from his father had been appropriate discipline.

In his third session, Ralph became emotional when he told about an incident that occurred several years earlier with his alcoholic older sister. When they were informed that his sister was considering suicide, Ralph and his wife drove to another city to be with her. They found her in "dreadful shape; she had hit rock-bottom." The following day, Ralph signed a form that committed her to a state rehabilitation center. Everyone had agreed, even his sister, that this was the best decision to be made. Months later, she came out of that center, and had managed her life reasonably well since then.

Nevertheless, Ralph was tearful as he told how he had committed his sister to this recovery program. Asked what he was feeling, he replied sadness and guilt. We explored the roots of his sadness and guilt and discovered underneath feelings of rejection and betrayal. Ralph was surprised to hear that the feelings of betrayal had less to do with his sister than with his own father.

When he committed her, Ralph felt he had betrayed her. Because of his own attachment to betrayal, Ralph identified with his sister and imagined that she was feeling betrayed by him. It was exactly these feelings of rejection and betrayal which, as a boy, Ralph himself had felt in connection with his father's treatment of him. He had completely repressed these feelings. "What's the point of looking into the past?" he had rationalized. "It's all over and forgotten." But the unconscious does not forget repressed feelings.

Ralph's secret attachment to rejection and betrayal had been covered up by guilt and sadness, which in turn were covered up by denial.

He had begun to act out with his son a repeat of his relationship with his father. Predictably, Ralph had begun to feel betrayed by his son. Before his son became a teenager, he idolized his father; as a typical teenager, however, he became more interested in his friends. Because of his problem with betrayal, Ralph found it easy to hold onto feeling injured by his son's apparent change of allegiance. Because Ralph was not aware of his own repressed feelings of rejection and betrayal, he could not understand his son's position or empathize with him. In being harsh and strict, Ralph was simply doing to his son what he himself had passively endured.

His repression of powerful feelings also cut down on the range of his emotional capacities, and he was unresponsive to his wife. At times, he had resorted to alcohol to cope with the vague inner misery brought about by the repressed and unresolved emotions.

Ralph was like a fear-filled dental patient, never relaxed about being in therapy. "People are often nervous about looking into their emotional problems," I told him. "There is a universal reluctance to examine one's psyche, because people are convinced they will find out they are bad or sick. This conviction is based on old childish fears of being defective, flawed, or inadequate. But the initial anxiety associated with self-discovery (the penetration of our defenses) is soon replaced by relief and a sense of well-being."

This next case also illustrates how secret attachments are covered over by secondary feelings and self-defeating behavior. Grace, an active bulimic, was fearful of her anger or anyone else's. She was convinced that she herself was a storehouse of anger. She had become remorseful after an emotional outburst in which she threw an object at a kitten that had scratched her.

"I would sooner go on with my bingeing and purging than hurt someone with my anger," Grace said, admitting that "it scares me."

She was convinced her anger would really hurt others, but this conviction was an exaggeration of the impact it had on others. She was unable to give specific examples of people or events which angered her, except to say that bad table manners irritated her.

Grace's mother had never expressed anger but, she said, "Dad was quite volatile, yelled a lot, spanked us, and disciplined us." Grace's mother had been very passive and afraid of her husband's anger. Grace claimed to be afraid of her own anger, but she was really fearful of anger itself because she would identify with the helpless and powerless victims of it (like her mother or the kitten she hurt).

The underlying problem (as it had been with her mother) was Grace's attachment to being powerless and helpless and feeling controlled and dominated by her father and his anger. In relationships, her tendency had been to become involved with men who, like her father, were controlling and dominating. Conversely, as a defense against being controlled, she was also attracted to "wimpy" men who were just the opposite of her father but with whom she soon became bored.

At one point, explaining why she was not in a relationship, Grace said, "I've been trying to get rid of everything in my life that might control me." However, her attachment to being controlled was being acted out insidiously in the form of her bulimia. Bingeing and purging was the manner in which she continued to be controlled by a powerful force. She felt powerless and helpless in the face of her eating disorder.

She saw bingeing and purging as her problem. The compulsion to binge and purge certainly got all her attention, but this self-damaging compulsion was covering up her anger, which in turn was covering up her attachment to the feelings of being helplessness and controlled.

Sometimes secret attachments are only partially hidden. For instance, a man who is very sensitive to rejection may know that this sensitivity is a weakness on his part. However, he is *not* likely to know of his secret attachment to rejection. He does not know *how* he secretly colludes in the creation of misery associated with feelings of rejection. He is especially *not* likely to know of his secret tendency to provoke rejection from others.

The feeling of shame is common in addictive personalities. Some addiction treatment specialists believe shame is the root cause of addictive behavior. But shame, which is the feeling of being exposed and punished, is a consequence of attachments to being humiliated and condemned.

Debbie, a compulsive overeater in her mid-sixties, was 100 pounds overweight and consumed by shame after overeating. "I have a poor self-image," she said, "and whenever I get into feelings about that I go and eat." Her mother had controlled her by making her feel ashamed, often asking in reprimand, "Aren't you ashamed?"

The family lived near a reform school, and the mother frequently threatened to send Debbie there for being naughty. One time, driving past the reform school, Debbie became hysterical in the back seat. To calm her down her father promised she would never be sent there. "I made up my mind I would never shame my own daughter," Debbie said, "so she got smacked instead."

Debbie had not escaped from encounters with shame. In fact, she shamed her daughter when she "smacked" her, and later, after episodes when she had been especially harsh with her daughter, Debbie would feel shame for these excesses. Debbie's attachments were to feelings of being disapproved of and condemned, and feelings of shame were a consequence.

The feeling of shame anticipates punishment. It denotes the expectation of being seen as bad, despicable, corrupt, and being punished accordingly. Debbie had not just pointed out inappropriate behavior, but did it in a way to make her daughter look bad. When Debbie brought the feelings of condemnation down on her daughter's head, she subjected her daughter to the same disapproval and shame that her mother had subjected her to.

There is a difference between talking about what happened as a child and getting into the feelings of it. When an individual gets into his feelings, and focuses on the passivity and helplessness he experienced as a child (rather than his actions and reactions), he understands more profoundly the nature of his secret attachments.

For example, one former drug user remembered frequently seeing his father bullied verbally by his mother. "I felt all alone, cut off from my father, and disappointed, let down, betrayed by him. I felt sick and sad and hopeless." As an adult, this man frequently felt disappointed and let down by others and then would feel sorry for himself as he indulged again in feeling let down and deprived emotionally. He benefited greatly as he connected with the betrayal feelings he had repressed and saw how he had been unconsciously holding on to attachments to betrayal and disappointment.

The circle diagram shown here illustrates the role of secret attachments and their impact in the life of an addictive personality. In the center at the deepest layer are the deep, hidden feelings to which we are secretly attached. In contrast, at the surface of awareness, the first layer represents the self-defeating and self-damaging behaviors that are both consequences of secret attachments and defenses intended to cover them up.

The middle layer consists of emotional reactions and more defenses (conscious and unconscious). These include anger, rage, worry, helplessness, frustration, guilt, insecurity, sadness, despair, urgency, dread, apathy, loneliness, hurt, craving, desire, anticipation, excitement, depression, self-condemnation, and so on. Often an addictive personality recognizes he has a problem with one or more of these emotions, but he does not begin to understand the origins of these emotions.

As stated, the origins are deeper in the unconscious, in an individual's secret attachments to certain negative feelings. Discovering these feelings and his attachment to them requires *insight* and involves a process of seeing and feeling the prevalent emotional experiences of childhood and correlating those with present feelings and behaviors.

For example, Delores gained insight into her relationship with her husband (he constantly belittled her) when she

Secret Attachments reside in the unconscious mind, covered up by defenses, emotional reactions, and self-destructive behaviors.

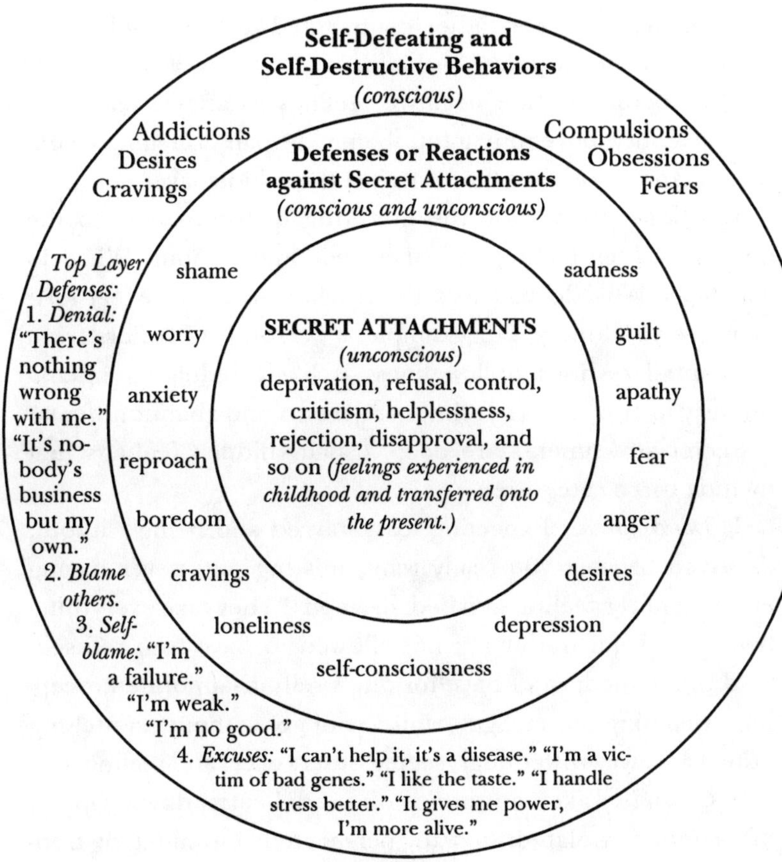

sensed how she had passively endured "put downs" from her alcoholic father who had belittled both her and her mother (who Delores had identified with). Growing awareness of her passivity (in this case, her attachment to being looked down upon, criticized, and seen as inadequate) enabled Delores to recognize how her unconscious willingness to play the role she experienced with her father contributed to the problems in the relationship with her husband.

Most people define negative feelings as anger, fear, sadness, jealousy, boredom, guilt, shame, despair, loneliness, confusion, and so on. But these are just the middle layer emotional reactions. Answering the following questions gets to the deeper, hidden feelings: What are you angry about? What do you fear? Why do you fear that? What makes you feel sad? Why are you lonely? For example, a person who suffers from substantial feelings of loneliness is likely indulging unconsciously in two deeper feelings–rejection and abandonment.

Secret attachments are deep, usually hidden feelings that include three categories:

1. *Deprivation.* Expecting loss; starved and being without; deprived of what you really want; missing out; never having enough; never feeling satisfied; drained ("They take everything from me, I get nothing"); not allowed to have fun; refused; held up; denied; can't have for one's self; disappointed; peeping (watching others get while you go without); watching others get away with things; seeing others excel and feeling less.

2. *Control.* Taken advantage of; used; beaten down; ripped off; conned; violated; lied to; persecuted; intimidated; trapped; forced to submit; pushed around; dominated; forced; restricted; inhibited; restrained; held up; made to endure inappropriate behavior; imposed upon; obligated; made to look bad; pick up the burden; do it all oneself; have to see things their way; told what to do; overwhelmed; helpless.

3. *Rejection.* Abandoned; betrayed; deserted; no longer im-

portant; not wanted; excluded; neglected; left out; looked down upon; put down; humiliated; insulted; criticized; judged harshly; not understood; not liked; hated; unfairly accused; disqualified; not recognized or acknowledged; seen as incompetent; ignored; not supported; not validated; let down; disappointed; can't trust or rely on anyone; seen as worthless, condemned.

Here is a technique or procedure to access hidden feelings:

A. Chose in your mind a situation that provoked negative emotions. Write down how the situation made you feel. Go beneath the anger, sadness, or whatever and describe what was done to you and how it felt. Use images, fairy tales, animals, or any other metaphors to describe your feelings. For example: "I feel like I'm struggling to keep my head above water." Ask how it would feel to go under. Or, "I feel like a discarded rag-doll." Ask what the doll would say if she could speak. Try to describe the victim feeling you experienced.

B. Take this feeling back into your past and describe childhood situations when you had this same feeling. Example: "Dad several times promised to take me to the zoo. But we never did go. He always had excuses. I felt disappointed, let down." Did Dad often promise and not deliver? If you cannot remember from childhood, recall similar feelings as an adult. Does this feeling represent a regular theme in your life?

C. Watch for a repeat of this feeling in your daily life. Do you look for it even when it is not there? Do you anticipate the feeling? Do you use situations to wallow in the feeling? Learn to recognize this feeling in your daily life and acknowledge how much you hold onto the feeling.

D. Recollect how you may have perpetuated the same feelings with others. This means, how may you have done the same to others that you felt was done to you. Example: "I, too, have disappointed others and let them down. I led Jane on to think I would marry her but pulled out at the last minute."

E. Describe how you do this to yourself. How do you shut yourself out and ignore yourself? Example: "I always tell myself I'm going to take a vacation—but I never do. Or "I'm always disappointed in my own achievements."

F. Try to sense your attachment to this feeling. Example: "Yes, I can see (or feel) that I am attached to the feeling of being disappointed and let down by others."

Most of our negative reactions toward others or events are due to transference, where the person replays and projects unresolved feelings and relationships from childhood onto his adult interactions with a spouse, children, friends, coworkers, strangers, as well as events or situations. (It is important to realize that transference is usually very subtle, in part because a great deal that passes in the way of communication between people is unconscious or subliminal. In a typical conversation, it has been suggested only twenty percent of communication consists of the words spoken. Perhaps forty percent of communication consists of tone of voice, emphasis, and inflection, and the remaining percentage is based on body language and facial expressions.)

The addictive personality, already carting around his secret attachments to deprivation, control, and rejection, stokes the fires of these attachments through transference and other unconscious perceptions. Unconsciously, he builds up the frustrations and resentments that trigger self-damaging behavior.

Remember that there is not necessarily a right or wrong in situations, just differing perceptions and reactions. Once a person breaks free of an attachment, he will have clarity and find solutions to his problems. Holding onto grudges and feelings of injustice only wastes energy and clouds judgment.

Before the point that you lose control and become self-destructive, monitor your feelings. As you feel yourself getting caught in negative emotions, be aware as well as you can of what negative feelings or experiences you are indulging in. Continue to observe yourself with this awareness of what it is you are indulging in. Even while being miserable and self-destructive, you can continue to see and feel your entanglement in your secret attachments. Doing this is an act of will that represents your determination to get better as well as the manner of achieving it. The following example shows how this can be done.

One of my clients was depressed and drinking more than usual because of his reaction to the recession and the drop in his income. "The recession is the catalyst for negative feelings that are your own," I said. "When your business slows, you get into feelings of being inadequate, no good, even worthless. You use business success as a measure of your own value. You need to develop the skill to catch yourself in the act of producing (in your mind or imagination) various negative thoughts, feelings, or scenarios involving your business. It is not easy to stop these negative impressions because very often the whole operation of producing these impressions is entirely unconscious. Other times, however, your involvement in the production of negativity is right there before your eyes, for instance, when you are actively producing thoughts or feelings that accentuate the conviction that your business is going to fail, and you will be seen as an incompetent or a failure. It is appropriate at such moments to say to yourself, "Why am I producing these negative thoughts and feelings? What's in it for me? I must really like doing this, even though it makes me feel so bad, because I seem determined to keep doing it."

"So you are saying," my client interjected, "that I should be trying instead to produce positive feelings and impressions."

"No, it's not so much that you try to produce the positive. The positive will take care of itself once you take care of the negative. Rather, you try to see and understand your unconscious determination to produce negative impressions of your life and the world. Try to see how you justify your determination to suffer. Try to see your willingness to react negatively to certain situations. The degree to which you react negatively is usually *not* justified by circumstances. Your negative reactions, as you experience them, are produced and maintained because a part of you has an agenda of secret collusion with feelings of failure and defeat."

This following case illustrates how difficult it can be to find one's hidden feelings or attachments. Joe, an alcoholic who was making excellent progress in his recovery, was falling in love. Despite the pleasures of this new relationship, he felt guilt and anxiety about it.

"Do I want to be this involved?" he would ask himself. "Is it too much, this involvement, this interaction? I don't feel I have enough room with her."

His guilt and anxiety were detracting from a relationship that otherwise was going well. Joe had a dream in which he was standing in a stilt house with an unidentified man. Suddenly, he spotted a large snake in the house, slithering along the baseboards from one room into another. Joe felt great fear of the snake and would not go near it. Eventually, the other man went up, grabbed it, and dropped it over the balcony onto the ground below. In the dream, Joe was "really upset" that he had been afraid. After awakening from the dream, he continued throughout that day to be upset for his alleged cowardice in not removing the snake.

To analyze the dream, we need to know a little more about Joe's life. He had a problem with feeling controlled. In his career, he became emotional when he felt that others were telling him how to do his work. During his alcoholic period, he had run-ins with police who represented to him controlling authority-figures. Deep down, his guilt and anxiety in the new relationship were caused by his unconscious willingness to indulge in feelings of being restricted and inhibited by the requirements of intimacy and the expectations of his girlfriend. As a defense to cover up his secret attachments, he pinned the guilt on something else, his alleged cowardice for not telling his girlfriend what he was feeling.

However, his girlfriend was open-minded and understanding and did not try to control or restrict him. He simply extrapolated this feeling of being controlled and inhibited from what he imagined was required of him in this relationship.

Joe was slinking (snake) around the house, not being honest. He believed that his problem was dishonesty and moral weakness, but this belief was a cover-up for his attachment to being controlled. The dream reinforced this defense, to believe that he was a weak coward. In the unconscious, to make the defense stick (or work), he was required to believe it to the point of suffering for it. And so he spent a whole day tormented by his alleged cowardice for not disposing of the snake, which corresponded with not being brave enough to tell his girlfriend how he was feeling. He had no inkling that under all of this lurked the hidden feelings, his attachments to feeling restricted and inhibited.

In another case, Sylvia, a compulsive overeater who had started therapy with me a few months earlier, realized in a session the power and covert nature of her secret attachments. She had become extremely agitated that week when she learned that her alcoholic son, in the throes of a nervous breakdown, had pledged to go into a treatment program. The son lived out-of-state and Sylvia had not spoken directly to him for several days.

"I should have been glad for him," she said, "but instead I was very anxious, even in a panic, with my heart racing and feeling just awful. I haven't been able to sleep, I've had intestinal difficulties, and I'm just on the run, like I'm frantically trying to get away from myself. I don't know what's happening, but I've been like this for three days now."

I deduced that she was identifying with her son, and feeling what she imagined he was experiencing. "What do you believe that your son has been feeling?" I asked.

"He must be feeling worthless, that he has failed again, that we're all looking down on him and seeing him as no good, and that we're fed up with him and his antics."

"These are the very feelings you get into with respect to overeating and weight gain," I said. "You disapprove of yourself and even condemn yourself when you lapse. I'm sure you love your son, but you're not identifying with him because you love him and want to protect him. Rather, you do so because of your own attachments to disapproval and feeling inadequate and worthless. You sneak in those feelings vicariously, through your son, in order to fulfill your own secret agenda."

"My God, it's true!" She began to cry. "I can't believe I do this. I can't believe it's so powerful. I don't know whether to be relieved to know this, or to be sad that this is what I'm doing." Five minutes later she said, "It's gone. Those anxious feelings are gone. Just like I burst a bubble. Thank you for this insight!"

Because of his decision to go into treatment, Sylvia's son might have been feeling very good about himself. But her unconscious did not necessarily deal with truth or facts. Sylvia's secret preference was to ignore all possibilities except the worst one that she could imagine, in order to feed her own attachments.

Once the secret attachments are revealed, and hence the hidden feelings, the connection to substance abuse or compulsive behavior can be very apparent, as in the following two situations.

One man, in recovery from alcohol abuse, drank three

quarts of whiskey over a long weekend, all the while feeling *helpless* in the grip of his addiction. In withdrawing from his friends and the outings he had planned with them, he also felt completely *abandoned.* Just before his binge, his car had broken down, leaving him feeling *helpless* without it and also *at the mercy of* auto mechanics to fix it properly at a reasonable cost. Also a few days before his binge, his girlfriend had abused him verbally, and he became entangled in feelings of being *abandoned* emotionally by her. His binge, an elaboration of his attachments to feeling *helpless* and *unloved,* served as a means to extend those feelings. "I was very much aware as I was drinking of how much I wanted to suffer and be hurt," he said.

In the other situation, a compulsive overeater who was struggling to diet and worried about her boyfriend's commitment to her, found herself unable to study for an important examination. She also dreaded having an anxiety attack when she sat down to take the exam. She was feeling *deprived* of food and love. Consequently, in being unable to study, she elaborated on the experience by *depriving* herself of vital knowledge; she was in a state of *not being willing to receive.* Because she was convinced emotionally of the great depth of her *deprivation,* she would not be inclined to sit down at an exam and display her *wealth* of knowledge. Hence, her anxiety about the coming exam.

For both these individuals, awareness of their secret attachments and a therapeutic approach to overcoming them provided the opportunities to recover from their conflicts and create positive outcomes for themselves.

In this last case, a man named Al came to see me because his recreational use of cocaine had become a daily habit. Together we set about determining the emotional and psychological weaknesses that accounted for his predicament—in other words, to find his hidden feelings.

At those times when he had not been using cocaine, he was hyperactive, rising before six in the morning and working hard throughout the day. A half-hour snooze in late afternoon perked up his energy, and he would be busy with activities and projects into the evening.

"When I'm feeling good," he said, "I have lots of energy, and I know how to get through the day. I have plenty to do."

He described his life in terms of *doing* things. When he was *doing* something, he felt fine. When he had nothing to do, he could become restless and easily bored. He liked it when time flew by or when he was "passing the time." For entertainment, he did push-ups or jumped in his car and went for a drive. At night he had trouble sleeping because his mind was buzzing with various agendas and activities he was planning.

"It looks to me, Al, that you have trouble just being comfortable with yourself, at peace with yourself. You need to be busy. Being active is fine, of course. But it looks like you depend on being active to avoid feeling what's really going on inside yourself. That's what you are doing when you jump in the car and go for a drive."

Al was most tempted, he said, to use cocaine in mid-to-late afternoon when his energy was running down and he felt depleted. When tired, his guard was down, and he was more likely to experience negative feelings, hence the desire for cocaine to boost his energy. When he was abstinent from cocaine, he often slept in the afternoons to recover his energy. For him, not having energy was more than a physical condition; it became an emotional condition. When tired, he tended to become apathetic and depressed, and feel drained or empty. He would slip into a deep passivity where he felt like nothing, without value, a nobody. In this condition, he lacked all motivation. His will turned to mush. In coping with that empty feeling, he sometimes ate more food, especially when he was cutting down on cocaine or when cocaine was not available.

In the beginning, Al had used cocaine to boost his ego in order to compensate for ways he felt incomplete and unworthy. Later, when the allure of ego-gratification had worn thin, he began to use cocaine to escape the nagging emotional reminders of his responsibilities. "Anything I had on my mind, I wanted to forget," he explained. "If it was a bill I had to pay, a job that needed my attention, something I had to do, then I was eager to forget about it all together."

Now he was trying to avoid another hidden feeling–being drained. Try as he did, he couldn't escape from that feeling with cocaine. Even increased doses of cocaine did not produce the same boost of energy he used to get. High on cocaine, he would lay around the house for days on end, doing nothing, absorbed in an unpleasant experience of profound passivity, feeling morose and useless, more than ever feeling drained just to get up and eat or go to the bathroom.

The single most important awareness in Al's working-out process was knowing those hidden feelings. He learned that his irrational or emotional side was tangled up in unpleasant negative emotions–feeling drained, depleted, and having no worth or value. An important part of this awareness was knowing that a side of himself did not want to let go of those feelings.

Here is a procedure, called the "worst-case scenario," that helps addictive personalities discover their hidden feelings and thus their secret attachments.

A. Write out your worst fears projected five to twenty years into your future. (Do not write what you want it to be–instead, make it a projection of your fears.) Example: "I still see myself struggling to make ends meet. I'm still not married. I'm alone, bitter. Everyone but me is happy."

B. Describe the feelings connected to each aspect of your

scenario. In what way are these feelings a pattern of your attitude toward life? Describe childhood examples of these same feelings. Example: "In childhood, my sisters never wanted to play with me." The feelings were isolation, loneliness, deprivation, sadness.

C. What are you doing or not doing to contribute to this scenario? Example: "I'm still not going out trying to meet people. I avoid friends and jobs that would lead to success."

D. Think of your five biggest fears or worries and write them down. For each fear, write a fantasy of the worst-possible scenario. Note the major feelings presented in each case. Sense whether you may be dwelling on each of these major feelings. Trace these feelings back to childhood. If the major feeling is loss, recall experiences of loss in childhood. This following statement reveals how an adult may experience this feeling: "I go on a trip and while I'm away I fear that my child is lost." The major feelings are terror, sadness, loss, grief, abandonment, helplessness.

Example from childhood: "One day our Dad took our dog to the pound without telling us. If I had been there I might have stopped him. I felt hurt, helpless, angry. I loved the dog." The hidden feelings in this last instance are helplessness and betrayal. Depending on the person, one of these two feelings may predominate in his life, or the individual may be struggling with combinations of the two feelings. Having these feelings means he is conditioned to experience them in different contexts repeatedly in his life—unless he understands the nature of this conditioning and works to free himself.

Without inner freedom, the emotional distress caused by the attachments and the need to defend against the attachments can lead him into addictive and compulsive behaviors.

Chapter 6

Roots of Secret Attachments

Secret attachments have their roots in the first eighteen months of life, the time known as the oral stage of development.

A primary problem of an individual's tendency toward addictive and compulsive behavior is the degree to which he is emotionally attached to the perception of himself as someone who never gets enough–a passive, helpless victim of others (initially mother) who refuse and deny him.

Let us visit a laboratory of orality to understand how this perception affects the behavior of the addictive personality. We will imagine you are a compulsive overeater, and for this laboratory I will use a restaurant.

1. *Waiting to be seated.* Maybe you are personally offended that a seat is not awaiting you, and that you have to stand in line for food. Deep in your psyche are memories of having to wait for Mommy to arrive with the breast or bottle. You hated that wait then and still do today. Unconsciously, though, it is what you expect, always waiting, always feeling deprived. Then, you get to the table and order, but the food is slow in

coming. (This is why fast-food restaurants are so popular. People hate to wait for food because doing so brings up those old feelings of neglect and deprivation.)

2. *Contemplating the menu.* The menu has numerous appetizing entrees, but if you pick the filet mignon, you can't have the baked shrimp. If you choose the chicken pot pie, you can't have the roast lamb. Some people agonize for fifteen minutes in choosing their meal. Unconsciously, such a person is consumed with the feeling of what he will *not* get after he makes his choice. Often he believes that his problem is *indecision,* but the deeper problem is his attachment to missing out. Instead of enjoying what he does order, he will be preoccupied with all the entrees he is *not* having.

3. *Not getting your fair share.* At last, after your impatient wait, the food arrives. However, you notice that your serving is not as large as you had expected. You glance around at the other plates. To your dismay, you see that your wife or husband, or even the children, have more on their plates than you. "Why look, they have twice as much mashed potatoes!" Wasn't that always the way it was when you were a kid? Didn't your brothers always get the bigger plates? Life's not fair. Instead of enjoying your meal, you slip into feelings of being gypped and cheated.

4. *Being disappointed.* Your meal does not taste that good. Your chicken pot pie has sour dumplings. "If only I had picked cabbage rolls instead. How could I have been so dumb! It is all the fault of the kids. If not for them, I could have gone to the health-food restaurant where the food is always perfect." Isn't this always the way it works? You sacrifice yourself and end up once again being deprived. And look, everyone else is absolutely loving what they got. How miserable should you become about this? Maybe you should say something about how bad the food is, to get a little sympathy at least.

5. *Paying the bill and feeling drained.* "Oh God, how much is

this going to cost? Why did I do this? I can't afford it. Things are so expensive nowadays. You can't even go out for a little meal without breaking the bank. Why does it always happen that whenever I try to have fun, something always spoils it?"

Most compulsive overeaters are unable to avoid slipping into some or all of the negative feelings just described. In such situations, the addictive personality has allowed his emotions to barge in the front door of his psyche like a pushy salesman. He needs to examine how and why he left the door ajar.

Oral issues persist in thousands of other ways. Examples include chronic frustration waiting in traffic lines or doctors' offices, being selfish or miserly, never satisfied in relationships, stuck in chronic boredom, engaged in excessive self-sacrifice, living in the past or the future instead of the present, unable to enjoy some product or experience because it is not quite "right."

In order to make sense of these secret unconscious attachments, it is important to understand a baby's experience of the first eighteen months of life. The focus of sensation in the first eighteen months is through the mucous membranes of the mouth, hence the oral stage. A baby also processes the new world around him on an emotional level and his emotional reactions are either pleasant, painful, or neutral.

Painful experiences are not necessarily a result of being mishandled by adults. For instance, a baby cries for the bottle or the breast. Now, he may have a very kind mother who nevertheless is in the kitchen cooking supper or taking care of other chores or children. She may not get to the baby for several minutes. But several minutes to the baby may seem like eternity because he has no capacity to understand the relativity of time.

So the baby comes to feel deprivation, a sense of not getting enough, a feeling of being refused and denied, missing out, insatiable hunger, and impatience. Over the years, as the baby becomes the child and then the adolescent, these unpleasant feelings can develop into dissatisfaction and disappointment with what he has, expectations of losing what he has, never feeling satisfied, or watching others get more.

Expulsion from the womb is accompanied by feelings of confusion, shock, pain, loss, and hard work. The baby must now suck (work hard) to get fed and to receive the nourishment which he used to receive automatically. He must cry loudly (another major effort) to let someone know when he wants to be fed. He feels deprived if his expectations are not met instantly.

In the beginning, the baby believes that everything (Mom and Dad, even objects) are extensions of himself. The baby's attainment of nourishment and attention are *not* seen as a result of mother's love but as a result of his own power and omnipotence. The baby's wishes are frustrated in many ways many times a day. The baby has a difficult time with this (as many adults do) because of the emotional conviction that he (or she) is the center of everything, all powerful, a little wizard or "Master of the Universe" who can expect and order compliance from everything around him. It surprises most people to hear that infants are possessed of this profound misconception of reality that psychology has termed egocentrism, or infantile megalomania, or omnipotence of thoughts.

Every disappointment is an offense to his extreme self-centeredness or megalomania. This produces frustration and fury that can be observed when he kicks and screams in temper tantrums. If the little child's wishes are not instantly met, as he expects them to be, he is bound to feel a sense of being deprived, neglected, refused, denied, and not given to. Because he knows no separation between his parents and himself, he becomes convinced that negative experiences and feelings are products of his own wishes.

Far from acknowledging his complete dependence on his mother, the child believes that he creates for himself, out of himself, everything that he wants and needs. It is important for the child, in preserving his self-centeredness, to believe, "I am not a passive victim but an active creator of the experience." So when he experiences deprivation or refusal, he feels he himself seeks and creates this experience. Even as reality begins to invade his little kingdom, the child clings to the illusion of being a wonderful wizard in the land of magical megalomania. The grasping of reality is a gradual process, which adults succeed at only in relative degrees.

In time, the growing baby becomes incapable of sustaining the fantasy of his own omnipotence. He begins to project that magical ability upon his parents and, later in life, upon religions, magicians, celebrities, medical doctors, or institutions. The growing child realizes he is less powerful than earlier supposed, and in fact that he is quite helpless to move about his environment and to demand things from it.

The feeling of helplessness lays the groundwork for the second major attachment that plagues addicts: the feeling of being controlled or dominated. (The first major attachment consists of feelings of deprivation, neglect, and refusal.)

Every child goes through a period of prolonged helplessness. His body has extremely limited mobility for several months. It may be more than a year before he walks. For years he cannot communicate effectively. Two decades may pass before he leaves home. Most other animals leave the nest or the lair to become independent within the first year.

Researchers hypothesize that this protracted helplessness is due to the sophisticated development of the human brain and nervous system. As a result of protracted helplessness, infantile traits and fears have a long time during which to become imprinted. This contributes to the degree to which humans are fixated emotionally to a past stage of their development.

In this helplessness, the child cannot make things happen. Things only happen to him. The tendency of some adults to be swept up by feelings of powerlessness has its origins here. Adults will grow up feeling helpless in certain contexts, for instance, helpless to influence government or bureaucracy, helpless in the face of the law, helpless to overcome diseases, helpless to refrain from certain behaviors, and helpless to control the consumption of alcohol, drugs, or food.

Through the period of protracted helplessness, the child has plenty of time to acquire in his unconscious an affinity for or attachment to (or to be conditioned to accept and tolerate) the feeling of being deprived, neglected, refused, rejected, criticized, controlled, or dominated.

These attachments are covered up by psychological defenses. Defenses include blaming ("She made me feel this way; if not for her, I wouldn't have a problem"); denial ("Who me? I don't have a problem, everything is fine"); excuses ("My parents didn't teach me that" or "I didn't say anything because I didn't want to hurt her feelings"); and projection ("You're the one who's angry, not me").

A person who is unconsciously attached to feeling refused or deprived (in a wide variety of possible ways) may defend against this attachment by too much consumption of food. The food binge not only compensates for an emotional emptiness produced by the attachment to feeling deprived, but also serves to prove (falsely) that he wants to get and be fulfilled (nourished) rather than to be deprived. The stronger the attachment, the more he defends and, in this case, the more he eats.

Emotionally, the addictive personality remains the hungry, demanding, starving infant who impatiently and unrealistically demands an ever-flowing breast. His impatience and inability to tolerate the frustration of delayed gratification is a protest to cover up his attachment to feeling neglected and deprived.

Because of this secret attachment to "not getting," addicts never feel satisfied, no matter how bountiful their lives may be, no matter how much their partners try to please them. They are like baby birds with their mouths stuck open, insisting on oral gratification while feeling they never get enough.

Addictive personalities are notorious for going after things or people they cannot have or which are out of reach. When they do "get," they quickly lose interest, become bored, and embark on other pursuits. They are attached and attracted to the "struggle to get" and not to the actual getting. The addict's secret agenda is to feel he is being refused or denied rather than being satisfied or fulfilled.

For instance, alcoholics regularly maintain an attitude of refusal. They refuse financial stability and emotional security to their spouses and children. They are extremely self-absorbed, trapped in the emotional conviction of how much they themselves are refused, and they consequently refuse to recognize or acknowledge the individuality and value of their spouses or children. In their inner conviction that everyone behaves as badly to them as the "refusing" mother of their infancy, they themselves become accomplished refusers. They refuse to see the pain they inflict on others. A primary source of grief for adult children of alcoholics is the degree to which as children they felt unrecognized and unappreciated around such parents.

There are many indications of attachments to oral deprivation that can affect so-called "normal" people, not just addictive personalities. One can feel deprived of attention, honesty, recognition, affection, sex, commitment, loyalty, and prosperity. In the unconscious, whatever one is feeling deprived of is incidental *to the underlying willingness to experience deprivation itself.* Unresolved oral issues create a desire for instant gratification and fuel the excesses of materialism. I believe they also contribute to social and economic problems such as the nation's low savings rate and chronic indebtedness.

Oral issues are also an obstacle to the development and mastery of skills. People who require instant gratification have reduced patience and tolerance for the rigors of becoming highly skilled in some field. You usually have to tolerate struggle and deprival for some time in order to master or create something substantial. A lot of people do not pursue goals because of the deprivation and struggle that is involved in the process of attaining these goals. Like infants, they want it now without any effort.

The following two examples illustrate experiences of deprival and refusal involving non-addictive personalities: (i) a family goes to a fast-food restaurant and the young son wants a dozen chicken pieces. His mother says that is too much, and orders him half that amount. The boy then throws a tantrum, and refuses to eat; (ii) a husband comes home from work to find that his wife, who has also worked all day, is tired and does not want to cook. She asks him to cook for himself, which angers him. That evening he pouts and complains and starves himself.

In both these actual cases, the experiences of refusal and deprival were clearly taken to unnecessary degrees of suffering. The individuals acted out the feelings of refusal and deprival beyond the initial disappointment of not getting. This is typical. The attachment to refusal and deprival can be so strong that once the individual gets the first taste of it, he feels compelled to experience it to a greater degree.

Oral issues can also get mixed up with love or what passes for love. In *Heavy Load,* a movie about compulsive overeating, an obese woman who is trying to diet purchases a box of donuts at a supermarket and becomes increasingly anxious about her purchase as she drives home. She pulls her car to the side of the road, takes the box of donuts and places it under the front wheel of her car. Then she drives over the box. She gets out of the car again, picks up the crushed box, and lovingly, as if carrying a baby, takes the box in her arms and carefully places it in the trunk of her car.

An overweight client who saw this film said this scene provided her with a major insight about her own relationship with food. For her, food was not only an obsession but "the only thing that gives me true satisfaction in life." Food for this single woman had become a substitute for "not getting" in a relationship. To consider cutting back on consumption meant the end of nurturing, the prospect of starvation. Her relationship with food was infantile because it paralleled her relationship with mother's breast, especially the infant's emotional focus on the breast as well as the reluctance to be weaned. Moderate consumption of food felt too much like deprival.

In the unconscious, food equals love. Food is associated with being at the breast and with the child's first experience of love. Overweight people often indulge in feeling rejected and unloved, and give food (mother's love) to themselves in compensation. Food is used for its tranquilizing effect, meaning its ability to repress the underlying emotional stirrings of feeling deprived, unloved, or rejected.

The client who saw the film said she had considered her "loving" relationship with food as a positive situation. The scene from the movie helped her understand that the relationship was infantile, not only limiting her personal development but also contributing to her overeating.

A similar kind of relationship can exist with alcohol and drugs. One alcoholic client said, "If you take away my booze, you take away my best friend." Another client, a habitual marijuana user, said longingly, as if referring to a lover, "I don't see how I could ever give up my pot." He added,

"When I've been without pot and I get some, I get a rush just from holding it in my hand. I get sexually aroused from the smell of it. I can taste that first suck on the joint." Giving up the addictions feels too much like deprival, even though in doing so the individual benefits in physical and emotional health.

In summary, addictions and compulsions are self-defeating reactions to one's unconscious attachments to feeling deprived, rejected, and a helpless victim of others who are felt to have all the power. The addictive personality's passivity mirrors the infant's helplessness and dependency on others who are felt to have all the power and control.

True recovery (not abstinence alone) is an ongoing process involving observation and understanding of one's present-day emotional reactions. This is done by 1) defining exactly when and how you experience a negative emotional reaction, and then identifying your specific hidden feelings in that situation; 2) taking responsibility for understanding your emotional reactions rather than focusing on what others are doing or not doing that upsets you; and 3) correlating your present emotional reactions with times in childhood that you felt the same way.

Gradually, your deepening understanding chips away at the secret attachments. Once those attachments have been undermined, serenity, clarity, and peace of mind follow.

Chapter 7

The Empty-Plate Disorder

"I'm beginning to see how, in every way, I set myself up to feel deprived," said 40-year-old Rose. The feeling started in her youth. When she was six, someone caught a rabbit and gave it to her for a pet. "You have to set it free," her stepfather told her, "but I will buy you a rabbit from a pet store." The pet rabbit, however, was never purchased. Rose never pressed her stepfather to fulfill his promise. But she never forgot the empty promise and passively endured the feeling of being deprived and let down.

The purpose of this chapter is to illustrate, through cases such as Rose's, more of the self-defeating and futile behaviors that result from the unconscious attachment to oral deprivation, neglect, and being refused. I call this problem *the empty-plate disorder.*

Another time Rose's mother baked a delicious pizza. Rose had a piece and then, with her aunt, went off for the afternoon. On the way home, she told her aunt she had only one piece of pizza and was looking forward to having more. At home, the aunt mentioned Rose's anticipation of the pizza to the mother. When the aunt left, the mother slapped her daughter hard across the face and said, "How dare you suggest to your aunt that you are being deprived!"

As Rose grew up, she was always a dieter but was never fat. In fact, she was anorexic for a period, and her weight fell from 105 pounds to 85 pounds following the break-up of a six-year romantic relationship. Very occasionally she would binge, which for her meant eating a box of cookies during the course of a day.

Rose's main self-defeating behavior, however, was to deprive herself through food, mirroring the deprivation she experienced in her relationships. She dieted even when she was underweight. She almost stopped eating completely for a few months following the breakup of her relationship.

Her loss-of-appetite reaction to rejection and letdown was the way she took control over the rejection and intensified her feelings of deprivation and loss. Unconsciously, she took this position: "I'm not passively attached to feelings of being refused, denied, and rejected. I'm bad, I do it to myself (stop eating)."

People with the empty-plate disorder go to the banquet of life to find their plates empty or, at best, filled with uninteresting foods that they do not want. Though they may consciously aspire to wealth, riches, and fame, they are effectively blocked by the unconscious condition of diminished expectations.

Seeing one's life as an empty plate becomes even more painful when contrasted with the plates of others that are heaped with all kinds of benefits and goodies. The unfairness of it all is played over and over like a refrain from a commercial jingle.

Karl Marx may have had empty-plate disorder. That would be true if he had been motivated to produce his economic theories primarily in an attempt to disprove an inner accusation that he was secretly attached to the feeling of deprivation when he saw (or imagined) industrialists reveling in their wealth. Marxists became fanatical in their allegiances to a tragically flawed social model, evidence of the emotional need to cover up the attachment to deprivation.

In other examples, the individual who compulsively wanders into the kitchen several times a day to peer into the refrigerator may be looking for what is *not* there in order to feel deprived. Men who are titillated by the presence of a buxom woman in a low-cut gown or a bikini-clad beauty on the beach may be playing with the idea of what they cannot see rather than enjoying what is exposed. An individual who several times a day compulsively checks on his image in a mirror is likely attached to the feeling of disappointment in what he sees. A peeping Tom might inwardly be after, not the sight of the naked woman, but the feeling of the woman's alleged refusal to show herself. (He has little interest in nakedness he can witness in an acceptable way.)

A child's reactions to deprivation can be seen in a thousand ways, and this childish part of ourselves remains active in the adult. A child may feel, for instance, that Mom and Dad never give him what he wants, that his sisters and brothers always get more. A child may have a temper tantrum because Mom cannot take him to a movie or because Mom did not buy the right kind of soda pop at the supermarket. Some children grow up to become adults who are always feeling dissatisfied, for whom more is never enough.

One woman, a compulsive spender, complained to me that her husband did not make enough money, that she was not able to make enough with her commissions as a saleswoman, that her furniture needed to be replaced, that her car was too old, that her home was too small. She had fears of becoming a "bag lady" in her old age because she worried there would not be enough funds for her retirement. Although she was bright and had great potential, she was limiting herself because of her attachment to deprivation. Her compulsive spending was a defense, designed to "prove" how much she wanted to get rather than to be deprived. The spending produced financial hardship, resulting in the deprivation she feared most.

"You're not as interested as you think in having more money," I told her. "Your life is being very strongly influenced by your unconscious priority, which is to re-experience repeatedly the feeling of being deprived and missing out on things."

She looked pained as she said, "It feels so awful to think that this is true."

"I know this is hard to come to terms with," I agreed. "This revelation of your secret attachments feels awful because it offends your ego, your sense of pride, to consider that some part of yourself is operating with so much control and so much against your best interests. Also, difficulty derives from a feeling that the therapy is taking something precious from you. It is taking something all right–your attachment to being deprived–which you unconsciously want to hang onto despite the suffering it causes.

"Enhancing our wisdom is a process of humility," I continued. "It is a matter of discovering how much we don't know. Well, one thing we know is that often the most foolish people are those who think they know it all. Discovering how much we don't know about ourselves initially may not feel good, but it is the way of self-knowledge and inner liberation. We see the resistance to this process with addictive personalities who often are denying their self-defeating behavior, though it is obvious to all observers."

Another client related an incident that happened during a vacation with her family. The children wanted to eat "their kind" of food and rejected their mother's restaurant choices. The mother felt deprived because she gave up what she wanted to satisfy her children. At the restaurant of the children's choice, she became morose, complained about the delays, felt nauseated, and generally became a bore. She chose a dish that she found quite unpalatable, making her suffering worse, while complaining loudly through her self-inflicted ordeal, unconsciously embellishing upon her willingness to be a victim. None of her suffering would have been necessary had she understood her unconscious appetite for deprival and had she chosen to refrain from bingeing on it.

In relationships, men and women are often compulsively attracted to others who are unavailable or unattainable. The bittersweet feelings of deprivation or loss are their real passions. When such people are faced with someone who is truly interested in them or available, they find some reason to reject him, often because he is "boring," meaning he offers no titillation to the unconscious passion for not getting.

A woman broke off her engagement with her fiance. She claimed there were too many flaws in his personality. And she was bored with him because she felt he did not satisfy her needs. A month later he found someone else, fell in love with that woman and decided to marry her. The first woman suddenly wanted him back and pursued him obsessively, with some of the fervor of the deranged female character in the movie *Fatal Attraction.* She felt betrayed, became enraged, and plotted ways to get even. With each phone call she made to him, she got more rejection. She fed upon this rejection and kept it alive within herself. Ironically, she really did not want this man all that much but was obsessed with him because he had suddenly become *un*available. "I realized all along I was in love with him," she claimed. But she was really attracted to what had become unavailable.

Others will look for what is missing in their partners' personalities and replay in their minds an endless litany of faults, flaws, and imperfections, dwelling on infinite feelings of disappointment and deprivation. Common laments that indicate indulgence in not getting, being refused, and expecting abandonment include, "He's not there for me," "He won't talk," or "If I tell him the truth, he'll leave me."

One woman was intent on finding the "Great Deprivers" in her life. To this end, she identified her husband and young daughter as the ones who were forcing her to work, depriving her of fun, requiring her attention, and costing her freedom. She reacted to this secret attachment by "running around" at night, drinking heavily, and using cocaine, "proving" how much she wanted to be liberated and free to do her own thing. Subsequently, she felt guilty for her "naughty" behavior, which made her feel even more resentful toward her husband and child. She noted ironically that she even resented the heavy workload in her office because it gave her no time to mope about feeling dissatisfied and sorry for herself.

Compulsive behaviors are often acted out in unhappy, if not destructive, relationships with spouses, friends, co-workers and supervisors. So called codependents, ("enablers" or emotional caterers) partake of the empty plate in the form of the emotional poverty of abusive or unsatisfying relationships. Some of the characteristics of this behavior are listed in the *Diagnostic and Statistical Manual of Mental Disorders (Third Edition-Revised),* under the category of Self-Defeating Personality Disorder.

The manual includes in this category those who compulsively choose people and situations that lead to disappointment or mistreatment, even when better options are available. The behavior is compulsive because the individual is conditioned to act it out in this self-defeating manner, and he is unable to make wiser choices until his attachments to feelings such as rejection and self-denial are being worked out. He is under the influence of unconscious priorities, a kind of secret agenda that has nothing to do with his well-being or happiness.

These individuals will reject or render ineffective the assistance of others. They tend to incite angry or rejecting responses from others, and then feel hurt, defeated, or humiliated. For example, a man makes fun of his wife in public, which provokes an angry retort from her. He is left feeling hurt and unjustly treated, but unconsciously he brought about this outcome with his provocation of her.

Freedom from this compulsion comes as the unconscious mechanisms and attachments to being refused, neglected, and deprived are repeatedly exposed to the light of one's awareness and intelligence.

Some individuals walk away from the banquet of life with empty plates by engaging in excessive self-sacrifice that is unsolicited by others and which seldom is reciprocated. This impulse to sacrifice oneself for another is called a *magic gesture,* a defense that covers up the attachment to deprival and refusal. This is the unconscious rationale or defense: "I'm not looking to be neglected. On the contrary, I want everyone to treat me nicely, just as I am so nice to others."

A woman with a graduate degree and a challenging new middle-management position was bound up in anxiety. Despite the thrilling possibilities of her new position, she felt threatened by her colleagues and supervisors.

"Some days, I'm convinced I don't deserve to be there," she said. "I feel I am not productive or worthy. I don't feel any confidence at all."

The slightest indication of disapproval from her boss convinced her that she was inadequate and worthless. This woman was compulsive in her search for praise and compliments because she had a secret attachment to feeling inferior and being seen as not good enough. Expecting to be validated by others, she was fated to come up empty. Getting praise or compliments was not going to solve her problem–it was like pouring water into a bottomless glass.

If an individual is secretly attached to rejection, he will behave in ways that bring about such rejection, i.e. by being jealous, indecisive, insecure. This behavior provokes the other person to do the rejecting. In this way, people bring about their own worst fears, as well as elicit the worst in each other.

Another indicator of the secret taste for "not getting" is a person's feeling that someone is out to take away his wealth, possessions, loves, or accomplishments. One wealthy client complained obsessively about how much his wife "cost" him financially, although he admitted that this cost was considerably less than he spent on himself for hobbies, travel, and entertainment.

He realized, in fact, that his negative emotions were illogical since his wife was relatively frugal. Nonetheless, he suffered every time he saw (or imagined) her spending a dollar, due to his secret attachment to feeling loss and deprivation.

This is similar to another negative emotion, the feeling of being drained or depleted. Often this attachment takes the form of excessive concern over money. One client, a prosperous businessman, obsessively counted the cash in his wallet several times a day. He especially felt this impulse immediately after he had spent a few dollars. He felt tired and anxious about not earning enough, despite his substantial wealth and income. Counting cash was his defense to establish how much he hated the feeling of being drained. When he recognized his unconscious attachment to feeling drained, and where it originated in his past, his symptoms–his anxiety and his compulsion to count his money–disappeared.

Compulsive savers deprive themselves on the pretext that they are saving for a rainy day. By doing without today, they claim they will have more tomorrow. Ironically, tomorrow never comes. The miser cultivates the feeling of being without, and maintains the charade by keeping tomorrow in the perpetual future.

An extreme case is the "pauper" who dies with thousands of dollars stuffed in his mattress. But the affliction is common—over the centuries religions have found millions of people willing to spend their lives in sacrifice and atonement, saving up their credits for promised rewards in heaven.

The feeling of urgency to get something, to have something, or the desire for an instant and immediate cure or fix, covers up some feelings of not getting or not being helped. The urgency or impatience is a frustration, a form of suffering that serves as "evidence" that one really does indeed want to get whatever it is he is secretly indulging in feeling deprived of.

As stated earlier, to binge on food is a defense, which for some addictive personalities represents an attempt to cover up their propensity for not having, for being refused or denied, or for feeling unloved. In the unconscious the defense is presented as, "I'm not looking for deprivation. Look at what lengths I go in order to get and to have. See how determined I am to make sure I do get, that I feel fulfilled." An individual would not need to stuff himself with food (representing love and nourishment) if he were not hooked on emotional starvation.

Substance abusers may say they are partaking of their substance as a reward for some behavior. Occasionally one will say the reward is due "for coping with the stress of the day." One compulsive eater said, "What's the matter with wanting to reward yourself? Isn't that a healthy thing to do?" But when the person rewards himself with something that is self-defeating, his action is out of balance and he has gone too far. What kind of reward is that? And where does this need to reward oneself come from?

It comes from the need to cover up or defend against some secret attachment. One woman made this comment about her boyfriend, who she said withheld affection and commitment from her: "I get the impulse to eat chocolate ice-cream after I spend some time with him." Her need to be satisfied with ice-cream covered up her secret indulgence in his emotional withholding and lack of commitment. "I want to get (this ice-cream)," her inner voice defended. "I'm not looking to be deprived emotionally."

Another defense against deprivation is exhibited by the garrulous person, the frivolous or compulsive talker. This person does not expect to be heard or taken seriously by others. He anticipates that he will be deprived of recognition and compensates by non-stop talking to draw attention to himself. However, he acts out his worst fears: the non-stop talking ensures he will not be taken seriously.

The idea that people can be addicted (emotionally) to the feeling of not getting or addicted to what they cannot have confounds our intelligence. Is it not logical that a child who feels refused when candy is repeatedly withheld will want to eat it to his heart's content when he grows up? As a child he might believe so. But as an adult he will most likely repeat the experiences of being "refused" in the new contexts of his adult life. For instance, a man who once did not get the candy might repeat the experience by expecting his wife to refuse his sexual advances. A woman who feels she was unloved by her father will be bored by men who are nice and considerate and will likely find herself attracted to cold, withholding types.

Because he is not expecting to get from others or from life, the addictive personality often behaves as if he has nothing to give. He is too preoccupied and caught up with his own feelings of deprivation and rejection to care about others. He tends to see the other person as a pseudo-mother, and asks, "What can this person give me and how can he benefit me?" Others are there to serve his emotional needs. He does not see people objectively, as individuals in their own right.

One client saw her relationships with men in terms of what they could offer her emotionally. She covered up her attachments to emotional deprivation with fantasies that her latest boyfriend "will really commit to me, and we'll go and live in his cabin in the Blue Ridge Mountains." Predictably, the men to whom she became attracted were either confirmed bachelors or, like her latest lover, married and therefore ultimately unavailable.

A more self-damaging experience of deprivation and rejection is despair. This is the experience of hitting rock-bottom, and some addicts have to experience its horror before they find the motivation to begin reform. The despairing person has sunk into the pits of his attachment to deprivation, helplessness, or rejection, into such bleakness that the consequent emotion is profound hopelessness. To linger in this black pit induces dreams of suicide, the ultimate self-aggression.

Often addictive personalities are cynical and critical, attitudes that keep alive the feeling of being neglected, deprived, or unworthy. A 20-year-old with drug and alcohol problems lived at home with his well-to-do father and stepmother. Although his father provided him with a home, car, a job in the family business, and paid his therapy fees, the young man had a cynical attitude and was intent on feeling deprived. He felt neglected by his father and misunderstood by his mother. An injustice collector, he refused to express himself and talk to them about his emotions and his grievances. Instead, he bottled up his frustrations, drank heavily, then went out driving one night and rolled his father's luxury car, luckily walking away uninjured.

He showed little remorse for his negligence and wanted to hold onto his emotional conviction that he was a neglected child. However, his therapy helped him see that his negative attitude was not justified by reality, but was due to childish elements that clouded his perspective (his emotional misinterpretation of circumstances). He began to understand how attached he was to his negative perception of life. He became more responsible and mature and cut back on his drinking.

Many addicts complain frequently that "things are unfair." These individuals can barely look around themselves without being struck by some aspect of the unfairness of life. Sometimes one will remark, "I know that things are not always fair–but it just doesn't seem right that I'm always the target!" This emotional attachment to the feeling of unfairness and deprivation persists beyond any logical thoughts to the contrary.

An addict is often a "doubter." He is always looking for contradictions and evidence to doubt the value of what is available to him. "I know it won't work," he quickly predicts. This person is attached to the passivity of not getting, missing out on something, watching life pass him by. He can guarantee this outcome with self-destructive addictions and compulsions.

Sharon, a 32-year-old woman, married with two children, came to therapy to try to alleviate her chronic unhappiness. She was a compulsive overeater, forty pounds overweight, with a preference for sweets. She had no career of her own and was easily bored when her children were off at school during the day. She started off her first session crying and talking about the death of her brother fifteen years earlier. He had been injured in a car accident twenty-two years ago and had remained in a coma for seven years until his death.

Sharon said her family became highly dysfunctional after the accident and during the years her brother lay in a coma. Her father became a workaholic, toiling long hours as an executive for a communications company, while her mother was "completely stressed" trying to raise the remaining five children and care for the household.

"Mother said Dad was an alcoholic, though I'm not so sure," she noted. "Certainly he was able to work and keep up a pretense of being okay." Sharon herself had shown alcoholic traits during her early twenties but had now stopped drinking except for the occasional beer.

"I'm full of anger," she said. "I missed out on a normal childhood. Why did Jimmy (her deceased brother) have to get in that accident! We've all paid for it. Why did I have to grow up the way I did, without the things I needed, without family support?" Sharon felt unable to give emotionally to her own children and to support their aspirations and activities. "I really love them and they're fine. But a lot of the time I resent them, and I have nothing to give them."

Sharon believed her best approach in therapy would be to ventilate her emotions, especially hurt, anger, and grief. "I have so much anger in me that I know has to come out," she said. "As a family, we didn't grieve properly for Jimmy. We didn't even talk about him. I've cried about him many times for years but it hasn't been enough. I have to go through the stages of grief, and I feel I haven't even started in the first stage yet!"

Ventilating her so-called anger and grief would only give Sharon short-term relief. Fifteen years after Jimmy's death, she was not crying for *him* but for *herself*. She was feeling sorry for herself, slipping into self-pity, indulging in being a passive, helpless victim of ill fate. Despite a decent relationship with her husband, and two fine children to share her life, she was consumed in chronic dissatisfaction. Her boredom was a clue that she was attached to feelings of deprival, missing out, not getting, loss.

Sharon believed her unhappiness resulted from what happened in her family following Jimmy's accident, but this was just an excuse to cover up her secret willingness to indulge in feeling short-changed. She wanted to believe she had missed out on a "normal" childhood and a chance to be happy. The anger Sharon felt was real enough. She did feel the anger, but it was a pseudo-protest that covered up her attachment to being a passive victim. "Look how much I hate my plight, how much I hate this feeling of missing out," she protested. Her anger covered up her secret attachment to feelings of deprival, loss, and missing out.

As stated, our present feelings and reactions are based on the significant emotional experiences that repeated themselves in our childhood. Everyone replays and projects these feelings (usually unconscious) onto others in his life. People create in their relations with friends, spouses, children, and co-workers a replay of their emotional experiences with fathers, mothers, and siblings. This tendency to transfer past feelings onto present relationships is especially heightened with addictive personalities. These past feelings, now mostly unconscious, have developed into secret attachments that represent an irrational part of the brain. Someone who, as a child, felt deprived and unloved by his mother, now looks to feel deprived and unloved by others in his adult life and will transfer this expectation to be unloved onto his spouse, friends, and children.

As he absorbs awareness of his attachment to being unloved, along with an understanding of its origins in childhood, the individual discovers he has choices to respond more appropriately. He learns *not* to take things personally, *not* to indulge in feeling deprived or unloved, and ultimately *not* to abuse substances or to behave compulsively.

Here is an exercise I gave a client that illustrates how this works. This man was reacting at work to feelings of being controlled and manipulated. "As you reflect on these feelings," I said, "go into your memory banks and recollect scenes from your past in which you felt controlled and manipulated. Was mother controlling, or father, or both? Or a brother or sister, or grandparents?

"In this exercise, become a little boy again in your imagination, and get a sensation of those old familiar feelings of being controlled. This is not a mental exercise. You try to *feel* this control fully in your body and to *feel* your passivity. Experience emotionally how the feeling of being controlled pervaded your childhood and continues in your adult life.

"It is extremely helpful for you to see how you transfer an old feeling from the past onto people and situations in the present. This awareness identifies the precise nature of your own involvement in your emotional difficulties."

Another important technique for eliminating secret attachments is to witness oneself from a position of detached objectivity while in the throes of an emotional reaction. Doing this is hard for many people but practice usually helps develop the ability. Let us say a person is caught up in an emotional reaction that is powerful and consuming. It is possible to establish an inner perspective from where he becomes a witness to his own emotional reactions. As a metaphor for this, imagine an army of liberation landing and establishing a beachhead in enemy territory. The army now has a solid base in enemy territory from where to conduct operations. In a comparable manner, an individual is able to establish an inner vantage point of objectivity and detachment in the midst of his emotional reactions, from where he can observe his unpleasant reactions to an event, a situation, or a person. Now he can say, for instance, "Wow! Am I ever angry (at myself, at this person, or situation)! Now where is this anger coming from? Why am I angry with this person? What do I feel he is doing to me? I'll just watch what's happening here and try to see what attachments inside myself have set me off like this."

From this perspective, the individual superimposes a rational impression upon his emotional or irrational reactions.

Now he has a whole new vantage point of strength from where to begin to see more clearly the nature of his emotional reactions so that he may minimize the suffering and the potential for self-damage.

For example, at a meeting with his boss Jack has an emotional reaction to a perceived criticism from his boss. Jack goes back to his desk and begins to reflect on his own emotional reaction rather than focusing on how cruel or unjust his boss is. As he looks into his own self, Jack begins to consider his emotional reaction in terms of how he knows he is quick to feel criticized. He remembers how criticized he used to feel by his father's remarks to him. He recognizes that he is indulging in criticism at this moment. He begins to see that he has control, that he can make a choice to cease and desist from that indulgence or, at least, to resist the temptation to indulge. This recognition of the nature of his secret involvement in suffering makes it possible for him to choose whether to continue to feast on the criticism or to let go of it. Even though his boss may indeed have been unfair, Jack does not have to binge on his attachment to criticism.

Often you will be so consumed in your emotional reactions that you will be unable to practice this procedure. You can go through this procedure later, when your emotions have receded, when you are able to apply rational analysis and self-awareness upon the recent event.

There are times when you will slip very covertly into an indulgence in some emotions, and you will be completely unaware that anything has happened until possibly hours or even days later, when your negative reactions pop up, often in completely unrelated situations. To apply this method, you must backtrack to see what experience may have set you off. (Often you fight your psychic battles on the wrong front. For example, an emotional reaction with something your boss said or did may not register consciously but will be experienced the next day as disagreement and conflict with your wife, and you become convinced that the problem is with your wife.) Ask yourself, "What happened recently to cause me to react like this?"

In the recovery processes described in this book, it is not that the individual necessarily has "to do something" to get better; rather, he has to "see" or understand specifically where his emotional reactions come from. Such insight in itself is very powerful. Insight gradually fortifies one's intelligence and prepares an individual to make choices that become the evidence of his new strength, peace, and inner freedom.

Chapter 8

The Battle for Control

The addictive personality often feels that his life is out of control. William, a client in his sixties, could not stop his midnight raids on the refrigerator, even after doctors told him his added weight endangered his life. These late-night raids were conducted after his wife had fallen asleep. She had been trying to no avail to control his weight problem with vegetarian meals. The more weight he gained the more insistent she had become that he eat only what she prepared for him.

Even if he fell asleep early, he would awaken at the allotted hour to prowl about the kitchen. Whenever he managed to refrain from raiding the refrigerator, he suffered from insomnia. Several times he had completed his midnight raids with hardly any awareness of what he was doing, almost as if he were sleep-walking.

I told William his underlying problem was his secret attachment to feeling controlled. He felt controlled and restricted by his wife, and so his midnight munching became a passive-aggressive defense to this effect: "I'm not looking to be controlled. Look, I do what I want. I go into the kitchen and eat and she can't stop me."

"Your defense is self-defeating," I said. "First, overeating endangers your health. Second, the more you gain weight, the more controlling she becomes toward you as she further restricts your diet and scolds you more adamantly. Third, you become increasingly helpless to the control and dominance of your compulsion. The more deeply you see and understand the origins and nature of your compulsion, the more it will lose its power over you."

Predictably, William left tell-tale signs such as crumbs and wrappers when he sneaked into the kitchen; so of course his wife knew he had been "naughty." This provoked her to try to control him even more. So William created a situation that generated the feeling to which he was attached (in this case, feeling controlled), while consciously he protested how much he hated the feeling.

William made an art of sneaking into the cookie jar. His mother had been a single parent, and he had felt especially constrained in accepting her authority and domination. Despite his conscious aversion to it, he acquired a strong attachment to this feeling of being controlled (having become accustomed to it), and this attachment haunted him in later life. His wife became a mother-substitute, and he acted out defiance against her by raiding the cookie jar, but at great cost to his health and happiness. (Coming under the emotional influence of food, as well as his submission to the midnight ritual, also were expressions of his attachment to feeling controlled.)

With this secret attachment, a person feels that when he is not in control of some person or situation, then he is *being controlled* by that person or situation. It is a case of either feeling the urgent need to maintain control *or* being out of control—with no room for experiencing the balance of these extremes. For example, a client who was an alcoholic constantly interrupted people talking to him. In ordinary conversation, he felt the need to "take control," and others saw him as obnoxious and pushy. In his mind, when others were doing the talking, they were in control. He felt the impulse to interrupt, to take over and shut them down, a kind of pseudo-aggression that covered up his passivity, his attachment to being controlled. His defense was, "I'm not looking to feel controlled; I'm the one who takes control."

Issues of control begin to surface when a child is eighteen months to three years old. The child has a tendency to resist toilet training and parental attempts to turn him into a social creature (socialization). Because of the child's self-centeredness, he or she is offended by having a parental figure telling him or her what to do and how to do it.

The "terrible twos," when children scream and protest against the feeling of being controlled and dominated, is a stage many parents find difficult. Even the kindest parents, who approach the task with gentle consideration, have children who feel controlled and dominated during this period of toilet training and early socialization.

Whether a child has controlling parents or not, he is still capable of cultivating the feeling of being controlled. If the parents are truly controlling, the child may have more justification for his objections to feeling controlled.

The feeling itself constitutes the passive experience of having to give up what you want and having to submit to, and go along with, someone else's will. The feeling is also experienced as obligations to carry out certain requirements or duties. As one client put it, "I'm always saying to myself, 'I *have to* do this, I *have to* do that.' It may just be the need to pick up some milk at the store, yet I make it feel like a heavy obligation. I feel I am being forced to perform this task. I can't just do it in stride. I make it a burden."

This is the experience of a person with a secret attachment

to feeling controlled. Such an individual easily slips into feelings of helplessness and powerlessness. He often feels overwhelmed and manipulated, and he is resentful of the role certain people play in his life. He will either be a rebel and resist authority, producing defiance to cover up his attachment, or he will allow others to direct and lead his life by passively following religions, institutional directives, ideologies, or other people. Often, as circumstances warrant, an individual will alternate back and forth between these extremes.

In the unconscious, it makes little difference whether the individual is feeling controlled by people, events, situations, the state, or circumstances—*or by the addictive capacities of certain substances.*

Addiction becomes a metaphor for the parental figure who continues to control the individual and have power over him. From childhood, the individual is accustomed to the feeling of a force presiding over his life. This does not mean that the force the parents exercised was cruel or inappropriate. Rather, it means the child experienced the power of his parents or guardians as a force controlling him, and acquired an unconscious attachment to the feeling of being controlled.

The addict is locked in conflict. His conscious part wants freedom, independence, and happiness, but the unconscious, infantile part remains expectant of, and attached to, feelings of being controlled by circumstances and passively forced to submit to the will of others.

The situation can be aggravated if the parents or guardians also had strong problems with control. One compulsive overeater in his fifties remembered having an English nanny who, when he was two and rebellious about eating, tied him to his chair and force-fed him.

Adults relate to the addictive substance as helpless children relate to their parents who have total power over them. The child's condition of protracted helplessness, discussed in the previous chapter, illustrates the conditions that enable the child and later the adult to be swept up in feelings of helplessness.

This helpless factor has been revealed in another context. In 1950, American psychoanalysts published a book, *The Authoritarian Personality,* based on analyses of people in Europe who had allowed fascism to grow and take over their governments. The passivity of these adults was associated with their unconscious tendency to be taken over, controlled, and dominated. The population of that era had been raised by parents who insisted on complete loyalty and obedience from their children. These parents were prepared to break the will or independent spirit of a child with severe beatings or other such punishments. The father's word was absolute, and many fathers were raving dictators of the family unit, while mothers were enforcers of the father's will. This type of family experience had instilled this generation of Europeans with a passivity that allowed for authoritarian models of government, with raving dictators at the head.

Hypnosis has an element of control and helplessness. The hypnotist is often an imposing figure with a self-confident manner, to whom the subject is willing to turn over his will and power. The appeal of vampire movies also reveals the attachment in succumbing to the spell of someone powerful, as does the reaction of the masses to the histrionics and emotional intensity of certain kinds of religious or political figures. An underlying fabric of life in the world's capitals is the inner urge to merge with power figures.

People watching TV can easily slip into the feeling of being "spaced out," almost "taken over" or possessed by the influence of the visual images. Addictive personalities often spend their evenings consuming TV programming with the same lack of self-awareness with which they consume the food or alcohol in front of them. They submit their will to the ongoing visual stimulus and, in this passive spell, they are more susceptible to their attachment to being controlled, and more likely to eat or drink excessively.

Not only do some individuals become addicted to a substance, they also behave as the incompetent, irresponsible child who forces the spouse or partner into taking care of them, as parents once did. An addict can feel even more controlled when the people in his life step in and take charge to reform his behavior. This illustrates how certain individuals, who protest and complain about being controlled or dominated, are unconsciously laying the groundwork for this very outcome.

"Is a person really powerless over his addiction?" one client asked.

"Yes and no," I replied. "Feeling powerless, helpless, and at the mercy of forces you cannot control are key components in addictive behaviors. You are acting out the feeling of being powerless when you surrender to the addiction and let it take over your will. You unconsciously choose to be powerless. The problem is not so much the substance but the influence you allow the substance to have over you. You give the substance the power to control and dominate your life. The answer lies in seeing how you give to others, as well as to the substance, the power to control your feelings, thoughts, and behaviors. It is as if you have an inner child who is attached to feeling controlled, dominated, and oppressed. This attachment is a carry-over of childhood helplessness when you felt yourself to be controlled and powerless under the domination of your parents. As an adult, you continue to act out a form of passivity, an affinity for helplessness, a willingness to be under the influence of some power as you felt yourself to be under the influence of your parents."

The substance a person is addicted to becomes a substitute for a parental or authority figure who the person perceived as controlling and dominating his will. Unconsciously, the addictive personality does not want to take charge of his life, be responsible for his own choices or decisions, or be responsible for himself. He is accustomed to submitting passively to the influence or will of others, although at times he resists this control with protests and rebellion and may have convinced himself that he answers to no one.

"You are only powerless," I told my client, "if you have attachments to the feeling of being controlled, dominated, and under the influence of people and situations. It is the attachment to being controlled that results in the loss of a sense of control, as well as a loss in self-esteem. Essentially, you are not powerless. You are making choices all the time, though many of those choices are made beneath your conscious awareness. An addictive personality makes an unconscious choice to render himself powerless to the substance to which he is addicted. Unconsciously, he allows people and situations to dominate, influence, and control him. Again, this is a reenactment of childhood passivity and helplessness with parents."

It is true there are many events and situations we cannot control or change. But we can learn to control our internal reactions to these events. We learn to be in control by gaining insight into our reactions. This provides a sense of inner power and composure, even though chaos may be rampant in people and events around us.

Some people want to believe they are powerless in the face of an addiction. This is their attempt to eliminate guilt associated with having an emotional problem. But they become more powerless because they are unwilling to face underlying emotional issues and be responsible for their actions and behaviors. Fortunately, a political and social movement is growing in America to have us assume more responsibility for our personal and national ills. We will not become winners by blaming genes or the Japanese. We have to assume personal responsibility for whatever is wrong in our lives.

Try to be an impartial witness to yourself. Become observant, and notice whether you hand over your power to other people or situations and allow them to direct or manage your life. Then consider carefully the ways and examples in which you felt controlled and dominated in childhood by your parents or siblings. In what ways as an adult do you feel controlled, dominated, and under the influence of people, events, and circumstances?

People do have the ability to live a balanced life. Balance is something an individual chooses for himself when he has self-confidence and learns to honor and respect his own integrity. A sense of personal power grows as we assume responsibility for the troubles in our lives. However, addicts secretly choose powerlessness as the condition of their lives.

Alcoholics Anonymous encourages alcoholics to turn their problems to a higher source ("Let go and let God"). The importance and value of AA programs is undisputed. However, the program shifts the unconscious willingness to be controlled away from dependence on alcohol to another power, what AA calls a higher spiritual power. Control by God is surely less self-damaging than control by alcohol. But emotional and behavioral problems persist when the underlying attachments are overlooked. As mentioned, substance abusers who manage to stop their addiction without getting to the roots of their secret attachments will be hampered in some other manner, usually in unsatisfactory relationships, job insecurities, nagging fears, or in various expressions of chronic dissatisfaction.

Problems of control are not exclusive to addictive personalities. One client, a professional aged forty, was handsome and articulate, but quite immature, even boyish in his manner. He resisted doing the paperwork required by his profession, saying he hated feeling forced to do it. Emotionally he felt that some conditions or elements such as legions of bureaucrats or "big, bad society" were forcing him to do paperwork. Of course, nothing was forcing him; it was simply in his best interest to do it. But because he felt forced, he rebelled through procrastination. This produced much unhappiness because he was, as he continued to procrastinate, prolonging his indulgence in feeling forced. Anyone who procrastinates to a self-defeating degree is in protest (defense) against the feeling of being controlled or forced.

Individuals can even feel controlled by physical ailments. One client who struggled with compulsive overeating and drug abuse had been experiencing a literal pain in the neck for more than seven years. Doctors said it was a pinched nerve and some had recommended surgery. He tried chiropractic adjustments, but the relief was short-lived. This pain was particularly severe whenever the client felt helpless and frustrated, when he would fall under the influence of what he called "the rage of being unable to alter circumstances." The pain in the neck was more than a metaphor; as a chronic ailment, it provided this individual with another manner in which he could slip into the feeling of being taken over, controlled, dominated, and helpless.

Jody, a compulsive overeater, felt resentful that she "had to go" to work five days a week at a bank. She decided to work part-time, three days a week. Soon Jody hated this because she was lazing around the house all day, either overeating or being tempted to. Once she understood her attachment to feeling controlled (forced to work more than she wanted), she returned to work full-time and felt good about it.

As a child, Jody had felt "very controlled" by a stepmother who required her to do a lot of housecleaning. At age thirteen, Jody weighed 160 pounds. Her stepmother "always pestered me about my weight." Feeling controlled by the stepmother, Jody had resisted unconsciously: "Don't tell me I have to clean house, and that I can't eat what I want. I'll do and eat what I want!" Now, when she felt controlled by the need to work for family income, or by supervisors at the bank, compulsive eating was her defense, her "evidence" that she was not passively attached to feeling controlled by someone and that she could do what she wanted. This defense provided temporary emotional release, but Jody soon felt controlled by her cravings for food. Of course, the defense of excessive eating is also self-damaging because of the health risk in gaining weight and because the quality of life is diminished.

A woman in her forties reported laying awake at night, obsessed with her work schedule for the following day. It made no difference whether she expected the coming day to be routine or exceptional; she lay in bed with her insomnia and relentlessly visualized the day unfolding, minute by minute, worried about unpredictable possibilities. "I run through the routine of the day," she said. "I have to get the day's activities straight in my mind. I'd like to get into the day and get it over with, but I have to wait."

This woman was imposing upon herself the feeling of being controlled and regulated. She laid in bed feeling dominated, overwhelmed, and drained by the requirements of her work-day agenda. She felt controlled by some unwritten law regulating her every thought and action. Without being aware, she was indulging in an attachment to feeling controlled. In defense or protest, she felt anxiety about her job and wished she could just stay home or, at least, do something else for a living. But there was no escaping her attachments–when she stayed home she started to feel controlled by cravings for food.

In order to learn more about their hidden attachments to control, members of a therapy group with eating disorders were assigned to write a letter to the part of themselves attached to control. One woman saw this part as a hairy monster with a huge gross mouth dripping with saliva and scum. "I kick at it, hate it, spit on it, yell at it, try to destroy it," she wrote. (This therapy technique allows a person to imagine the nature of the part that has control. The person can speak to that part, say how it makes him feel, and then intuitively listen for its reply. The technique reveals the stance the individual takes with a secret attachment and the nature of the interaction.)

In this case, the woman was repulsed by the image yet fascinated by it. She felt herself building up her rage toward this "monster," which persisted for a few moments before she lapsed into passivity, into a feeling of being overwhelmed and controlled by it. This interaction revealed a frequent pattern in her life, to protest against some power or influence in her life and then eventually to give in passively to it.

One client felt this control in the supermarket. "I have to avoid certain aisles because it feels like the food talks to me," she said. "I feel it saying, 'Take me, take me!' I feel like it wants to jump into my cart."

Another client, Helen, a successful businesswoman who had recently retired, came to therapy to seek help for her addictions to cigarettes and alcohol. Helen revealed she was controlling with her sons, one of whom had bought her home-decorating business. She was trying to guide her other son through his own tangled business affairs. She could see her controlling influence in their lives, but felt justified because she was "helping" them.

"I just feel they would mess up if I wasn't there checking up on them," Helen said. Her controlling behavior, however, was a defense against her attachment to watching someone fail and feeling helpless to do anything about it, as well as a defense against her willingness to be drained by taking on the burdens of other people.

Helen acted out her own passivity and expectation of failure through her inability to stop smoking and drinking. She also unconsciously expected other people to look at her and see her as a failure, and she projected this onto her sons, expecting them to fail. She then identified with their helplessness and felt compelled to rescue them.

Individuals who easily slip into helpless feelings often have fears around taking action and making decisions. One alcoholic client, in therapy with me following an in-patient five-week treatment program, said in his third session, "I've been out of the treatment center for two weeks now, and I'm not liking the feeling of being back in reality. I'm not liking dealing with work, and making decisions about finances, and having to do something about problems in my marriage. I feel like a little child trying to do an adult job." That statement revealed that the helpless feelings that had led him to drink in the first place were starting to haunt him again.

Often these individuals will feel it is important to put up a strong front and to look as if they can handle anything. One such person told me, "Knowledge makes me feel powerful and is a great source of satisfaction." People who fall into helplessness often will try to look powerful on the surface or to feel powerful. But this false front collapses under pressure.

Sometimes, in more severe cases, what addictive personalities call their "disease" becomes an expression of the only act of will they have. This happens to those who feel they have a fatal flaw, something intrinsically bad or wrong about themselves that cannot be redeemed. The "disease" represents a form of autonomy. If their "disease" is taken away, it feels as if they must surrender themselves to some other person and be overwhelmed by the dominance of another. They feel on an inner level, "At least there's something here I am in charge of, acting out my disease."

The addict thereby establishes a feeling of autonomy by acting out with substance abuse or compulsive behavior. The claim to power is declared, "I made myself bad. I cause you to see me as bad. See, you can't control me." Trapped in this mentality, the addict does not have the power to succeed, but only to fail. For many addicts, this is the only way to defend against the attachment to being dependent, the attachment to being forced to submit to the will of parents or others.

This unconscious configuration produces the "dependee" personality often associated with addictive personalities. The dependee is someone who maneuvers himself into a position of dependence on others and ends up complaining about and being disappointed in the "inadequacy" of the provider's care. The dependent one is plagued with feelings of being incomplete and impotent but blames others for not doing their job and taking care of him properly. Underneath, this individual is turning his life over (submitting) to someone who lets him down and fails to save him from himself. The dependee acts out the baby, still not responsible for himself, wanting Mommy's constant care and attention.

To cover up the attachments to control and refusal, the defense of blaming is invoked: "See what you made me, Mother. See how screwed up I am because of your inadequate care. I wouldn't be an alcoholic if you had taken proper care of me." This defense is unconscious; the addict is only aware of his bitterness and resentment toward the parent-provider figures who he is convinced are responsible for his failures.

The addict will feel a need to dismiss or reduce those who want to help him. He loves nothing more than to make them confess to their "inadequacies." Behind this is his own expectation of being invalidated, to feel emotionally castrated by mother. He feels like a "nothing" compared with the "all-knowing" superior mother-figure. The protest is, "Mother (provider) doesn't take me seriously. She doesn't acknowledge me–she dismisses and diminishes me." Or "I'm not a complete failure who doesn't want to take care of himself. They have done this to me by not taking proper care of me."

One addict, feeling crushed by some off-the-wall remark by his mother, said, "I can't help it–she robs me of my soul." This is the ultimate rationalization for helplessness and the continuation of addictive behavior: "I can't help my behavior–Mom took away my spirit."

Addicts become emotional dependees, placing not only physical well-being but also their emotional well-being in the hands of others. One compulsive overeater told me that as a youngster she often ran to her mother for consolation when kids had excluded her at school. "I depended on her to help me emotionally, but it didn't work. She tried, she said things would be okay, and I would be all right, but it didn't get better for me."

An addict may be entangled in several attachments. For instance, an alcoholic may start out his drinking career because of an attachment to feeling deprived. As one alcoholic observed, "At first I enjoyed the alcohol so much because I got such a high from it. I felt so good, so light-headed."

In this first stage of his addiction, the alcohol was used as a defense to "prove" that he really wanted to get the most from life, that he really wanted that wonderful high feeling, when in fact he was unconsciously aligned with inner emptiness, deprivation, even lifelessness. Alcohol became vitally important to him to cover up his attachment to his inner inertia or emotional deprivation. Later, when this person had been using alcohol for some time, he became physically addicted to it. Now he succumbed to the feeling of being taken over, possessed, dominated, and controlled by the power that alcohol had over him, while becoming increasingly apathetic and lifeless.

This individual was also displaying an attachment to rejection; the more inappropriately he behaved when drunk, the more he could anticipate and get rejection from family and friends. Finally, when he hit bottom, he had degenerated or regressed into a helpless condition. Like a baby, he needed others to take over his life, get him into treatment, and back on his feet again. His whole life had to be taken over and controlled by others.

A healthy individual enjoys the good things in his life as he strives to make his life even better. But the substance abuser is attached to the feeling that something is missing, whether it is power, recognition, happiness, fulfillment, love, or material things. He tries to fill that void with alcohol, drugs, or food–or behaves compulsively–or is both addictive and compulsive. He is trying to escape the hunger, loneliness, and boredom in his life. But recovery from substance abuse, *and including the prospects for happiness,* depend on uncovering the roots of his discontent.

Drug addicts often say they take cocaine and marijuana to relieve boredom, to heighten a sense of aliveness, to enrich the imagination, to feel more potent, and to get "more" from life. "I want excitement, fun, bliss," they say. Drugs can accomplish all of this but only temporarily–and with dire consequences. Addictive personalities are under constant inner pressure to have fun or to feel ecstatic in order to "prove" that they are not secretly attached to being refused, denied, and deprived. Under the influence of cocaine, an individual experiences a kind of fascism of the ego that promotes the illusion of self-importance and personal power, restoring the old feelings of self-centeredness so prized by the addict's emotional (irrational or infantile) side. The individual uses the drug's "high" to compensate for underlying attachments to feelings of powerlessness, helplessness, worthlessness, and inadequacy. The drug addict subsequently ends up being even more helpless and powerless as he is "taken over" or "possessed" by the drug.

Some addictive persons, often the more educated or sophisticated addicts, claim that drugs help in seeking spirituality and union with God. This is cosmic escapism. These individuals feel adrift, empty, without purpose, and they use drugs to provide feelings of spiritual aliveness. It is attachments to deprivation and emptiness that burden them with emotional convictions that life is not good enough and does not give them what they want. They protest their attachments to feeling deprived and refused by claiming, "No, not true, I want nothing short of cosmic union."

Their problems are not with spirituality but with reality; they are unwilling to come to terms with how they perceive and respond to conditions in their lives. It is also a contradiction to claim some higher good will result from use of a psychologically and physically debilitating substance.

The most self-defeating expression of helplessness is suicide. Shame, guilt, and depression have all been proposed as causes of suicide. But these emotions are the consequences or symptoms of the despair of powerlessness and the emotional conviction of worthlessness that have their origins in *both* biological anomalies and the experiences of childhood.

A healthy person is in control of his life, yet he does not feel the need to control events or others. In contrast, a person with a control problem feels the need to control, and he can be quite unpleasant in his insistence on getting his way. The controlling individual feels the need to impose his will or wishes on others to cover up inner feelings of helplessness and powerlessness. He secretly expects to be controlled by others, and his controlling behavior is a defense against this.

"Let's control them before they control me" is his defense.

For example, a wealthy individual in his fifties felt that his wife was manipulating and controlling. He had married her a few years before and had become convinced she was after his money. He became enraged during any discussions about money or challenges to his authority, treating her coldly, calling her names, threatening to leave her, compulsive in his attempts to control her. Yet, in his business dealings he bailed out financially irresponsible partners who mismanaged company assets. He lost money in many such rescue attempts, but never complained or exhibited resentment directly toward these partners. However, because of the human tendency to fight unconscious conflicts on the wrong front, he would transfer to his wife—who actually was quite responsible and frugal—the feelings of being taken advantage of, manipulated, and controlled.

Brad was another client with an attachment to feeling controlled. He reported drinking excessively in order to relax. He felt pressure from the duties and obligations of his work and home life, and he said that drinking seemed to be tied in with his procrastination on important assignments. As a boy his strict and dominating mother had required him to carry out many of the farm chores. Brad had felt she forced him to act against his will, although in reality the chores did have to be done and he was the logical choice to do them. He internalized his mother's commands and, as an adult, experienced an inner voice that made him feel guilty when he was not doing his "chores." This way he became his "own" mother to himself, making himself feel forced to do chores.

To defend against this secret attachment to feeling forced, Brad resorted to drinking to provide this defense: "I don't look for the feeling of being compelled to work. On the contrary, I try to relax with a few drinks in order to forget all the things I'm supposed to do." Excessive drinking was his defense against the attachment to feeling forced. His self-defeating behavior was apparent in declining health, potential loss of income, and guilty feelings about his drinking and procrastination.

Addictive personalities have experienced feelings of being caught, condemned, or reprimanded for a variety of forbidden behaviors as their parents made such demands as: "Don't play in the street! Don't swear! Don't eat food in the bedroom! Don't eat sweets before dinner! Don't jump on your bed!" Many people have experienced the thrill of doing something "naughty" and being found out. The anticipation or thrill of being caught is often a major inducement to have extra-marital affairs.

One client with a history of alcohol and drug abuse was concerned that her father would think less of her if he ever found out she was also bulimic. He was a successful businessman, and she was convinced he would look down at her and see her as incompetent, weak, unable to handle things, a failure in her life. On the surface, she desperately wanted approval from her father. But anyone who is desperate for approval is unconsciously attached to disapproval. Her inclination was to provoke her father to think less of her and then secretly revel in the feelings of shame and condemnation she was attached to from childhood. After psychotherapy, which addressed this as well as her attachments to deprivation and control, her bulimia became inactive.

Another bulimic, Lori, created a pattern of being "naughty," then punished, and then finally forgiven and loved. She remembered that as a little girl she was paddled on the buttocks by her father. Whenever the baby-sitter told her parents that the children had misbehaved during their absence, she and her sisters were lined up in the order they were born and paddled.

"This spanking happened often," Lori said. "We were real

little hellions." After the punishment, her father lavished them with love and kind words, saying the punishment had been necessary but that he regretted having had to do it. As an adult, she behaved as if she could only be loved, or accept love, once she had been punished or abused. She engaged in self-abuse, and often binged and purged in the evening while her husband was at work. Then she would punish herself with guilt, self-loathing, and recriminations. Finally, in tears she would call up her husband and tell him what had happened. He frequently rushed home to console her and love her. This punishment-versus-love pattern was strongly ingrained, and Lori's bulimia was a convenient means to act out her attachment to it.

Notice in the following example how the unconscious switches from one experience of being controlled to another. Janine's husband, a generous but authoritative personality, died when she was in her mid-sixties. In the following three years, Janine gained fifty pounds before seeking treatment. "I guess I turned to food for solace and fun," she said.

In fact, Janine unconsciously missed her husband's controlling personality and turned to food to provide herself with another variation of feeling controlled. She was conditioned to seek a force outside herself that she felt exercised control over her. With her husband dead, her compulsion with food became the means to experience this control.

"I'm so strong with everything but food," she said. "It's frustrating, I try to have control over everything."

Janine would become angry at herself for "lack of discipline," believing that this deficiency was her primary problem. She was pleading guilty to a lack of discipline, and paying the price in self-recrimination, in order to cover up her attachment to feeling controlled.

People can subject themselves to a feeling of being controlled when they misuse or overuse the word *should.* "I *should* be nicer; I *should* stop doing this; I *should* have done that." Misuse of the word, or "shoulding on yourself," subjects an individual to inner dissatisfaction with himself and the feeling that looking over his shoulder is some observer who disapproves of the way he conducts his life.

A nineteen-year-old boy was managing to torture himself with the word *should.* He was anorexic and living at home with his divorced mother. The boy's refusal of food represented a "refusal of mother" and was a passive-aggressive defense to cover up his passivity, in this case a secret attachment to being controlled by his dominating mother. His anorexia caused serious health problems, and he had been admitted to hospital several times. The mother was emotionally insecure and required her son to behave in a manner defined by her. Unconsciously, she did not want the boy (who looked no more than sixteen) to grow up. The boy indulged in being controlled and dominated by her and was secretly thrilled by her intense though negative preoccupation with him. To deny his attachment to feeling controlled by her, he tormented himself with thoughts that he *should* try harder to please Mommy and to be a nicer boy for Mommy's sake.

But such sentiments were in vain. He was compelled to act out his self-damaging defense based on this rationale: "Mother doesn't control me. On the contrary, I refuse to eat her food. She can't make me. I even control her feelings and get her upset. True, she doesn't like me behaving like this, but a least I am responsible. It is *my* compulsive behavior that is controlling her." This claim-to-power defense covered up his secret willingness to indulge in feeling controlled but produced much guilt and shame for being "naughty" and a disappointment to his mother.

Sometimes individuals resist psychotherapy because receiving from others brings up feelings of being dependent and controlled. In order to get something of value from parents, some children feel they have to submit to another's authority. As adults, getting or receiving becomes associated with ego-reduction, humiliation, and submission.

The child received the "bounty" from all-powerful parents who appeared to give only when they felt the child was passive and obliging. Thus, receiving is associated with being manipulated and rendered helpless, at the mercy of the giver. The better the help and advice, the more controlled or reduced the child can feel.

Some addictive personalities associate commitment and marriage with submission to another's authority. They feel controlled and reduced by their partners rather than seeing and enjoying the positive benefits they can receive in such relationships.

A man who had a dominating mother grew up accustomed to being dominated by her. He was attracted to strong women but, through his defenses, began to withdraw emotionally and behave coldly when he felt controlled or pushed around by them.

He married a forceful woman and had trouble dealing effectively with her. Secretly, this man was expecting and seeking out experiences of domination. At times, he did act more assertively with her, but usually in a reactive, angry manner. This "pseudo-aggression" was no solution for his attachment to control and domination. Later, his defenses shifted. Instead of behaving coldly or aggressively toward her, he compulsively began to keep secrets from her. This was a revised attempt to "prove" he did not like being forced by her to account for himself. However, holding onto secrets for this purpose blocked intimacy between them. His wife became suspicious about the reasons for his secretive manner, then alarmed, and this made him even more accountable to her.

Some addictive personalities resist recovery because they

associate getting better with *bending to the will of their parents or society.* Addictive behaviors become a rebellion against the parents and what the parents expect their children to be (or what society expects and requires). It feels to the addict (in this passive-aggressive reaction to the feeling of being controlled by the parents) that he is defeating the parents. True, he may be bringing pain to his parents, but he is only defeating himself.

An individual is inclined to accept self-defeat when he can claim he is doing it to himself, to avoid recognizing a secret attachment such as his passivity to being controlled. It is like a prisoner who takes a cyanide tablet so his enemy cannot hang him: "Yes, it's true, I die either way. But at least I do it to myself."

Only individuals who inwardly feel powerless, helpless, and unworthy need to exert power over others or bend them to their way of thinking or living. An individual with self-confidence who feels in charge of his life, and who can give to himself, does not need to impose his will or his ideas on anyone else. He does not need power, he already has it.

Many power-seekers, ideological fanatics, busybodies, or meddlers are addictive personalities. They slip into the role of a dominating parent and try to control others the way they felt controlled as children. They do to others what they felt was done to them. Most people who need to control others have unresolved control issues with their own parents or siblings. They have not resolved the offense to their egos of being dominated by their parents. They have a passive streak that makes them prone to addictions and compulsions, even while they are compensating for their sense of helplessness by asserting power over others.

The need to control others also represents an attempt to control oneself, that is, one's own emotions, thoughts, and behaviors. Controlling others provides the individual with an illusion of being in control of himself. "I would feel out of control," a client told me when I asked her what it would feel like not to control others. Since her sense of self was weak, controlling others gave her not only a defense but an identity, a purpose.

Ask yourself in what areas of your life you feel controlled (with job, spouse, children). How did you feel controlled by parents or siblings?

The following personality traits indicate you have an attachment to feeling controlled, dominated, or manipulated. In brackets are the controlling influences you will encounter as a result of your passivity.

1) Can't say no (then others will take control).
2) Can't make decisions (others make them for you).
3) Seek out answers from others (let them control and manage your life).
4) Often feel impotent (fate will take over your life).
5) Fear of being assertive (allows others to take over).
6) Blame others (feel dominated and manipulated by them).
7) Feelings of failure (circumstance, not you, is in control).

Begin to observe yourself entangled in feeling helpless and controlled, and sense to what degree you may passively be indulging in those feelings. Try to realize that you have a choice to either succumb to feeling controlled or to resist the temptation to give in to the helpless feelings.

Chapter 9

Looking For Rejection

Victor came to psychotherapy after a month-long program at a treatment center had stabilized his bulimic-anorexic eating disorder. He had started using street drugs and alcohol at age fourteen, stopped using "chemicals" at age nineteen, and quit his heavy drinking at age twenty-seven. After a blackout on a drinking binge, he quit alcohol completely at age thirty, but had then transferred his substance abuse to food.

Victor's parents had separated when he was nine years old and divorced when he was fourteen. His parents had fought and quarrelled viciously from the beginning of their marriage. "They married on a dare," he said, "and then they ended up staying together because their own parents wanted them to get the marriage annulled." Victor started to eat heavily just as his parents separated, and at one point, at a height of five feet, two inches, he weighed 210 pounds. As a teenager one summer when he was heavily into drugs, he went from 210 to 145 pounds because he was determined to be accepted by the "bad" crowd he fell in with.

As a child, Victor felt isolated and abandoned. "My parents

weren't expressive, I didn't get a lot of affection and comfort from them," he said.

Victor's father, an engineer, had worked long hours and had given him minimum attention when at home. After the separation, his mother became more interested in boyfriends and frequently left him alone with his older brother. During this time his older brother was verbally abusive to him and called him by one name exclusively, Fatso. Both he and his brother, he said, were now having substantial emotional problems as adults.

He had felt "misplaced" at school. "As I got heavier, the kids really teased me. I would binge from the time I got home from school late into the evening, watching TV and eating until Mom got home." He had done well in school until he was about twelve, then he lost interest, skipped classes and got into trouble with teachers.

"I hated the school environment, not so much the classes as the other kids."

Victor's primary problem had its roots in feelings of rejection and abandonment. From an early age, he had interpreted his parents' deep unhappiness and general hostility to life as personal rejection of him. Even when his father had been in a rage at Victor's mother or furious for some other reason, Victor nevertheless saw the look on his father's face and felt father was hating and rejecting him. Because of the family's instability and the degree of marital strife, Victor also felt substantial insecurity and prospects of abandonment.

As a young adult, Victor's personal appearance was extremely important to him. He was desperate to maintain an ideal body weight. This was his defense against an attachment to being rejected and abandoned: "I don't expect or want rejection. Look how hard I work at looking good." Thus his eating disorder became a means of regulating his weight. He had stayed within a ten-pound range of ideal weight in the year before starting therapy, but his bulimia created great emotional distress, and he could feel control of his life slipping away.

He generated anger when he sensed people being "demanding and impolite" to him. This anger was also a defense against his attachment to feelings of being disliked and overlooked by others (the anger was served up as evidence that he detested the feelings of being disliked and overlooked). "They're not thinking about me," he remarked of his friends and co-workers. "They're just out for themselves."

Rejection and betrayal are themes that come into prominence when a child is three or four years old. At this age, the child becomes energetically and emotionally–even erotically–attracted to the opposite-sexed parent. At times, he feels he wants to possess the parent, to win the parent's attention exclusively, and have the parent all to himself.

A little girl, in longing for this emotional bonding with her father, may feel that "Daddy loves Mommy better than he loves me." And a little boy attracted to his mother may feel, "Mommy loves Daddy better than she loves me." A child might also see his siblings as love-objects of a parent, and therefore competition for the parent's love. The child takes personally the feeling that Daddy and Mommy are not loving enough in return. The child can then begin to harbor inner feelings of being unloved, rejected, betrayed. The situation for a child can be much worse when a parent is cold, withholding, cruel, or abusive.

Very often, people who were adopted as infants or toddlers have a major problem with rejection, as if they had undergone some powerful experience of original parental rejection or abandonment.

This stage of growth is the time of "two's company, three's a crowd." The child can feel like an outsider, left out, pushed aside. This is also when the child can feel reduced, degraded, devalued–and he may sense his parents saying, "We don't want you." In compensation, emphasis may be shifted to performance to win approval or acceptance ("See how good I am"). A lingering effect of this period is jealousy, the feeling of losing out to another. People with major unresolved emotions from this period sometimes have affairs, recreating "two's company, three's a crowd."

The addictive personality repeatedly misconstrues reality in a way that fulfills attachments to rejection, betrayal, and humiliation. His encounters with others are processed through his unconscious attachment to rejection. His ability to be offended by apparent indifference or hostility toward him is marked by an emotional intensity that is out of proportion to the facts.

An individual attached to rejection often perceives hostility where none exists and grossly minimizes his own aggressiveness. Like a gun loaded with distorted perceptions, he sees his aggressiveness as justified, a way to protect himself from others out to get him. His revenge or punishment for suspected transgressions against himself seldom fit the crime. His retaliation may be several times more severe and exaggerated.

Such individuals often indulge in feeling unloved. Annette, a bulimic, had felt isolation and abandonment in her childhood. Her two brothers and two sisters were several years older, and she felt they had ignored and overlooked her. She believed she had not been planned nor wanted as a child. Now in her mid-twenties, without romance in her life, Annette came home from work and invariably began to feel lonely. "There's no one here who really loves me," she often thought. Whenever she secretly began to indulge in feeling unloved, she created an emotional hunger and then experienced a powerful craving for food. Food and love became synonymous in her unconscious mind. Both represented giving to herself, caring for herself, and nourishing herself.

(Loneliness is a negative emotion that serves as against, or reaction to, the attachment to feeling unloved. The unconscious defense works like this: "I am not secretly attached to feeling unloved. Look at how lonely I am. That proves I want to be loved.")

Annette had another emotional complication, an attachment to being seen in a negative light. She could feel criticized just in being seen or observed by others. She imagined others would, without exception, find her body to be unattractive and unacceptable. She hated the thought of gaining weight and feared rejection. Throwing up or purging became her means of weight control and the self-destructive consequences of her attachment to rejection. Meanwhile, she lived in fear that others would find out about her bulimia and scorn her and reject her for it.

Most addictive personalities have an attachment, often quite profound, to being seen in a negative light. They expect to be regarded as inadequate, not good enough, or inferior. They are focused on an image of how they look to others and often provoke others to judge them negatively. This provocation is a defense called negative exhibitionism. The addict is seen in a negative light when he gets drunk, acts "goofy" on drugs, becomes obese, or acts the fool with some compulsion. The inner defense now says, "I'm not attached to having people look at me with scorn and disgust; I cause it to happen with my bad, out-of-control behavior."

Addictive personalities do not need someone else to judge them or condemn them; they readily become their own worst judges. They whip themselves mercilessly for being inadequate and "bad," rejecting themselves more harshly than anyone else rejects them.

Addictive personalities often become secretive, hiding their addictions or compulsions from others. In their secrecy, they are focused on what others would think or say if their behavior became known. The secrecy is now a defense: "You see, I hide what I'm doing from others so no one will know, no one can find fault or judge me." Bulimics often are horrified at the prospect of being discovered and dwell relentlessly on the possibility. Their anxiety indicates the intensity of their preoccupation with being seen and judged.

Another client, Joanne, behaved compulsively with food and diet pills from age sixteen to twenty-seven, even though she had a slender attractive figure that only fluctuated a few pounds during this period. Her father, who had been remote and indifferent to her, had been overweight himself and obsessed about it. He tried numerous diets and always failed with them. He transferred his own tendencies toward self-disapproval onto his daughter and once offered to pay her $100 a pound to lose weight, even though her weight was normal. "I always wanted to be thinner," Joanne said. "When I was in college I was always checking out the other women more than the men, to see how I compared physically with them."

Her desire to be thinner was prompted by her conscious wish to please her father who, she felt, would like her more if she lost weight. Unconsciously, however, she expected her father to reject and disapprove of her and not accept her as she was. Her obsession with her weight diminished when, in her late twenties, she began a business career. At that point, she transferred her expectation of rejection and disapproval onto her bosses and, as a defense, became a workaholic determined to please them with her dedication and total commitment. Several years later her obsession with food and weight reappeared after a boyfriend offered her $1,000 to gain several pounds because he felt she was too skinny. Although she did not want to put on the weight, she felt in conflict because of her emotional need (defense) to please.

"You wouldn't believe the amount of energy I invest to

make sure everyone approves of me and is pleased with me," Joanne said. She felt trapped in a no-win situation. Despite the energy she expended, she remained worried that someone, anyone, might reject her. The more compulsively she sought approval, the more she anticipated rejection.

Healthy individuals are not emotionally dependent on being liked. They have enough self-esteem that such validation is not required for them to feel good about themselves. They have no need to cover up or defend against a secret attachment to feeling rejected. They understand that if someone does not like them, it may be because that person is projecting upon them his own unresolved emotions. To get to that comfort zone, you have to see how much a part of yourself is willing to feel the blast of an A-bomb from a powder-puff of rejection.

Leonard, a middle-aged businessman, was depressed and feeling guilty, resulting in heavy drinking. He had recently experienced betrayal by business associates and was extremely bitter. He also had a pattern of being betrayed and rejected by women. In analysis, he revealed that he felt betrayed by his parents, especially by what he perceived as their withdrawal of emotional support during his adolescence. He told the story of how, when he was about ten years old, his father persuaded him to "squeal" on some friends with whom he had broken into a canteen and stolen sodas and chocolate bars. The father apparently had made the boy feel that "father's love" would be the reward for this confession. But after the boy had told on his friends, the father betrayed the boy (or so the boy perceived) by failing to deliver the "love."

Leonard had acquired a secret taste for the feeling of being betrayed and was, therefore, a prime candidate to experience it repeatedly in his life. He became involved with individuals who, while pleasant on the surface, were untrustworthy. He acted naive and overly trusting of them, providing them with confidential business information they used to their own advantage. He also saw how he provoked women to reject him, mainly through his jealousy and withdrawal.

As Leonard realized his own secret collusion in acting out his attachment to betrayal, he stopped blaming his former partners. Even though they had indeed betrayed him, he saw that his anger and blame were inappropriate because he had secretly been "setting himself up" for such an experience. His best strategy was to understand these past occurrences so he would not blunder again into this type of trouble.

He had also been blaming himself for his alleged unpleasant personality and inability to sustain friendships. But this self-blame was also a defense, covering up in another manner his attachment to being rejected and betrayed. "I'm not looking for rejection," he protested. "Rejection just happens because of my unpleasant personality." The self-blame, with which he had to punish himself to make this defense effective, was a contributor to his depression: he was required to feel bad about his alleged unpleasant personality. Once this defense was penetrated, Leonard eased off on his drinking and was able to sustain and enjoy new relationships.

The addictive personality, caught in cycles of recurring self-damage, is inclined to see himself as a victim of circumstances or others. He believes his happiness is contingent on changing someone else's behavior toward him, in getting a better job, in making more money, and so on. When something bad happens to him, he will observe, "I was just walking along innocently when a brick fell on my head." But this individual has cooperated in his misfortune. To use the example of the brick, it is as if he saw a construction sign reading, "Danger, Keep Out!" but nonetheless walked into the danger, tempting fate.

The pattern of self-destructive behavior in many addictive and compulsive personalities proceeds in the following manner. First, the addictive personality unconsciously provokes, misuses or misinterprets a situation in which he perceives that someone or something is unjust to him. Second, not seeing his role in initiating his predicament or in embellishing his reaction, he feels victimized or offended. Third, caught in an emotional trap of recrimination, bitterness, retaliation, defeat, and withholding, he sinks into a negative vortex of self-pity, self-reproach, and self-hate, as he augments his deepening emotional crisis with addictive and compulsive behaviors.

Oscar, a middle-aged man who had been on an emotional-disability pension for more than a year, came to counseling at the urging of his wife. He had become emotionally unstable a year earlier after the death of his parents, both in their eighties. His parents had died within a week of each other in the same hospital. This man had doted on his father and mother and telephoned them daily from his home more than 500 miles away. His wife had also come in for therapy, complaining of his obsessive and irrational jealousy.

In his dress and bearing, Oscar resembled an overgrown teenager; he was lacking in grace, poise, and dignity. He was living on his disability pension, trying to reconcile with his wife who was now threatening to leave him because of his jealousy and increasingly erratic behavior. He was tormented by hatred for doctors and hospitals, and had been attempting through politicians and the press to hold an inquiry into the deaths of his parents. He was seeing a psychiatrist once every few months to maintain his disability status, as well as for drugs to treat his anxiety and digestive disorders.

Since the death of his parents, Oscar had lost his career, become seriously ill, made what looked like an unwise move to a new locale, and was about to lose his wife. Yet he tried to devote the three sessions he attended (before ending his therapy) to reciting with emotional intensity his litany of grievances against the world, especially doctors and hospitals. Nothing mattered to him emotionally as much as proving how justified he was in his disenchantment with life.

Oscar's relationship with his parents had been "close" because he had been trying (on the surface) to get love and validation from them. His wife had complained of how "he lived for his parents." His mother, however, had been quite negative, cold, and withholding. Unconsciously, he was attached to the feeling of being unloved and unrecognized—by his mother especially. When his parents suddenly died, his entire defense system collapsed (his means of "proving" how much he wanted to be loved), and he experienced an emotional breakdown.

In the next stage, Oscar was consumed with rage against doctors and hospitals, ostensibly for "killing" his parents but really for "killing" his defenses. With his parents gone, he had begun to look to his wife for rejection, and flew into a rage (as a pseudo-aggressive defense) when she offered a soda to a telephone repairman who had come into their house.

This next case also illustrates the consequences of an attachment to rejection. Marion, a woman in her fifties, was a cynic and heavy drinker who had been unable to develop a solid relationship with a man. She felt that, as a child, she had been displaced by her younger brother; it had appeared to her that mother liked her brother better. This colored her attitude toward her mother, and she blamed her mother for a multitude of alleged transgressions. She saw her brother as depriving her and she felt shut out. In her resentment, Marion emotionally shut out her mother and brother, while she acted out with others her expectations of deprivation and rejection.

Marion realized she could begin to experience her brother as a source of pleasure and fun, not a liability. Her feelings toward her mother and brother, she now realized, were a reaction to her secret indulgence in feelings of deprivation and rejection. Even if it were true that her mother had preferred her brother, Marion saw that spending her life as a victim of this happening was highly inappropriate and completely unnecessary. In this moment of insight, she began to understand her emotional misunderstanding, that she was secretly invested in seeing reality from a point of view of refusal and rejection, and she was able to ease up on her lifetime of resentment toward males.

An addictive personality, in his litany of complaints, tries to enlist sympathizers, bolstering his "right" to suffer. He hopes his listeners will validate his perceptions of how wrongly he is being treated, and bestow upon him the love, acknowledgment, and approval he consciously wants but unconsciously does not expect to get.

In one case of obsessive worry and speculation, Darlene learned from her boyfriend that he still talked occasionally to his former girlfriend. Darlene began to grow anxious, imagining that her boyfriend still wanted the other woman. However, she refrained from seeking clarity and did not press him for a forthright report on the status of that relationship.

When he would leave on a business trip, Darlene imagined him meeting his former girlfriend. She examined the phone bills looking for calls to this woman. She pouted, cried to herself and gave him the silent treatment to punish him for his alleged crimes. Her indulgence in the fantasy of rejection and betrayal went on for months. Yet she avoided confronting him with her feelings, and refrained from direct questions concerning his past relationship and how he felt toward the former girlfriend. She said in therapy, "I just cannot seem to confront him; I'm afraid he'll say he loves her."

That was exactly what Darlene was unconsciously attached to hearing. When she finally did confront him, he explained the nature of the former relationship to her satisfaction and assured Darlene he loved only her. "My God," she exclaimed later, "why did I put myself though all of that torment?"

In another case, a client's mother used to tell her repeatedly, "If you have sex with a man, he won't want to marry you." This woman had an attachment to the feeling of rejection and, in acting this out, was unmarried and unattached in her forties. She was deeply troubled about the timing for having first sex with a new boyfriend and, though she claimed to dread the event, she would often become compliant and seductive to facilitate it. Once intercourse had occurred with a man she cared about, she became needy, demanding, and jealous. In fact, she unconsciously used the first experience of sex with a new boyfriend to rekindle her attachment to rejection. In her words, "Everything is okay between us until I have sex, and then I become grim and demanding and end up driving him away." This woman was unconsciously making use of her mother's words to facilitate her feelings of rejection and to heighten her sense of being a victim of her mother as well as of men.

Being overweight is often a consequence of an attachment to rejection. Sarah, a twenty-year-old who was one hundred pounds overweight, had a date to have lunch with her father. She got to the restaurant ten minutes early, and found herself beginning immediately to feel that he would be late or would not even show up. Soon she was in emotional agitation and was looking over the menu with an increasingly ravenous appetite. Her father showed up ten minutes late, and Sarah could hardly bring herself to be civil to him. She ate a big meal and insisted on a high-calorie dessert, sensing his disapproval for her excessive consumption.

As a child, Sarah came to the emotional conclusion that her father did not love her enough. Indeed, it appears he was quite inattentive to her, which made it easier for her to have become attached to the feeling of rejection. He often kidded her about getting "chubby" and several times such remarks sent her crying to her bedroom.

Sarah had come to counseling because of compulsive overeating, as well as timidity and lack of self-confidence. She had dropped out of her freshman year at college because of acute loneliness and insecurity. Although she had been using cocaine, she had stopped at the time therapy began. Her mother, who was attractive and slender, and her father, also good-looking, were separated. She lived with her father who, during her childhood, had frequently made note of his interest in attractive women but was not attentive to his pretty daughter.

Sarah's inability to control her impulses to eat produced feelings of guilt. She then punished herself with reproach and self-loathing for being out of control with food. By getting fat, she extracted more indifference and also disapproval from her father.

Several times Sarah had lost 20 or 30 pounds. At that point, she became anxious about how to handle relationships, now that she was becoming more attractive. She associated a relationship with the example of her parents, and identified with her mother who, she felt, had been "unloved, controlled and cheated on." As she came up against her own fear of rejection (a fear caused by her unconscious attachment to rejection), she found herself beginning to overeat and put the weight back on. She was using her obesity as a defense against her attachment to rejection: "I'm not looking for rejection," her defense protested, "I am rejected because I'm fat and I'm unable to lose the weight." To make matters worse for herself, she was also using food to compensate for her indulgence in feeling unloved.

At one point, she moved out of her father's home into an apartment with two other women. These other women were quite popular and were out most nights with boyfriends. Sarah had difficulty controlling impulses to eat when she saw the other women having fun, enabling her to feel more deprival by comparison. She also indulged in feeling rejected when her friends did not take her along. She realized that the more she felt hurt and deprived, the more passive she became, and the more likely she was to remain at home feeling sorry for herself.

Jack, a client in his fifties, became entrapped in compulsive overeating after he gave up alcohol abuse. His primary problem concerned rejection as well as control. His father had been a "drunken bull-headed tyrant" who frequently beat him.

"I never wanted to raise my kids the way he raised me–but I did," Jack said regretfully. "I became the same monster to them that he was to me."

His sister and even neighborhood kids were treated cordially by the father, while Jack was so neglected he had to sleep on a couch or a cot all his childhood days. Later, as a salesman, he would drink too much and overeat when a sale fell through because he took it personally and indulged in being rejected.

One time after his father had beaten him, he told his father, "Goddamn it, you never let me do what I want to do." He remembered that, from ages ten to fourteen especially, he was always being grounded and restricted by his father. "I couldn't breathe when he was around." Although he was not brought up in any religion, as an adult he joined a strict traditional church.

"I was attracted to that church because it told me what to do, how to think and believe," he said, agreeing that this choice was influenced by his attachment to the feeling of being controlled. Later, Jack joined another church that was even more controlling. Finally, in what was still another defense against feeling controlled (this time at the other extreme), he joined another religious organization that had no special requirements and said he could believe whatever he wanted.

Another client, Tish, was a bulimic who had a rejection problem with her father. "Whatever I did was never good enough," she said. "If I got ninety-eight on a test, he wanted to know where I missed on the other two points."

After losing considerable weight in a treatment program, she still rejected herself by continuing to reject her body. Her negative body image then centered on the excess skin left from her overweight condition. It was her secret attachment, not the excess skin, that posed her emotional problem: even with a more appealing body she would find an imperfection to use against herself. Unconsciously, she made use of a complicated defense called a *negative magic gesture*. In the unconscious, the defense is presented with ironic bitterness: "I am not attached to rejection. I am only doing to myself what Mom and Dad taught me. They rejected me, now I am doing to myself what they did to me, only more so." To enhance the sense of victimization, the defense elaborates, "Through my self-image I want everyone to see what my parents did to me, how bad it was for me, and what I had to endure from them."

June, an alcoholic who also had an eating disorder, said in a session that she hated her body. She recalled that her mother had been on a variety of diets and had battled against her overweight body, constantly frustrated by her inability to stabilize her weight.

Following a relapse during which June had binged and purged, she said in a session, "I'm angry at my body. It betrays me, I have no respect for it. It's always wanting food, never satisfied."

In detesting her body, June was rejecting herself, as she had felt rejected in her childhood by her mother. Like her mother, she was also attached to being controlled and dominated (feeling helpless), at the mercy of forces she felt she could not control. A typical recurring thought was, "You have never been able to control your eating in the past, what makes you think you can do it now?" June also had a significant problem with deprivation and was easily caught up in feelings of losing out or missing out.

Sometimes a person indulges in rejection or some other negative feelings by identifying with someone else. You may find it easy, for instance, when listening to a friend who is complaining about life's injustices to identify with that person's feelings, experiences, and perceptions, and to start feeling victimized yourself.

One client, Arnold, was a habitual marijuana user with a secret attachment to feeling rejected. One day at the beach he saw a drunken male fawning over a group of young bikini-clad women. The women scorned and rejected the drunk. Arnold became enraged and had to resist an impulse to collar the drunk and run him off the beach.

In his unconscious he had slipped into the drunk's shoes (identification). Feeling what he imagined the drunk was feeling, he secretly indulged in rejection from the women as if he himself were being rejected. His anger toward the drunk was a defense, a cover-up designed to "prove" how much he hated the feeling of rejection in which he was secretly indulging. He had to pay a price for his defense, and that was to suffer with his anger and later to indulge and reinforce his weakness for marijuana.

Another client, Vicki, was a workaholic who said she became depressed after learning that a co-worker's husband had died of cancer. She related that this death had made her begin to think a lot about her father's death many years earlier.

The emotional impact of his death, she said in a session, was "the realization that he really loved me and now he was gone."

Vicki had indulged for months in the feeling of being abandoned when her father died, and now years later she was able to rekindle that feeling by identifying with the co-worker and imagining or embellishing upon the degree of abandonment that woman might be feeling following her husband's death. Vicki's depression was a price she had to pay for becoming emotionally entangled (through her co-worker) in her own secret attachment to feeling abandoned. She immediately felt better when she realized how and why she had been identifying with her co-worker, and this insight helped diminish her attachment to abandonment.

Many addictive personalities become mired in anger. The anger is a reaction and a defense against their indulgence in perceived injustices. Unconsciously, they are willing to prolong the indulgences in their secret attachments. So they stay angry and then they resort to addictions and compulsions as another self-defeating consequence of their energetic manufacture of negativity.

Exorcising the anger requires more than saying, for instance, "I forgive her for rejecting me." Forgiveness implies that serious offense has occurred. Yet often the offense consists of little more than the "victim's" flawed impression of rejection or exaggerated reaction to it. Insight and understanding is required in this situation, not forgiveness.

Blake's albatross was anger. A thirty-year-old bartender, he succeeded in becoming abstinent after he entered a month-long program at a treatment center for alcohol and drug abuse. His treatment followed a suicide attempt. Although he remained abstinent, he again became depressed and suicidal a few months later and began therapy with me.

Blake was tormented by what he perceived as his parents' rejection and disapproval of his homosexuality. His parents and other family members lived hundreds of miles away, and he refused to accept letters or gifts from them or to return their phone calls. He admitted they were reaching out to him and trying to show love, "but if they can't accept who and what I am, I won't have anything to do with them."

Nevertheless, he could not shut them out of his mind. In his imagination, he kept returning to old scenes from years ago when his sexuality had been "exposed" and he had left home feeling shamed and disgraced. He had a tendency now to brood for hours on all the ways he felt unloved, rejected, and disapproved of by them.

"The depressions you have been experiencing," I told him, "are a direct result of your unconscious tendency to indulge in these feelings of being unloved and disapproved of. The bitterness and anger you have been feeling toward your family are also direct consequences of your emotional willingness to hold onto feeling rejected and disapproved of. The bitterness is like a negative charge inside yourself. It can flair up at any time and put you back in an emotional state where you are contemplating suicide. There is a way to extinguish that negative charge, although it will feel to you as if you are losing something precious.

"You agree you are better off without the negative charge. To eliminate it doesn't mean you have to begin to love your parents. It means, however, that you at least become neutral toward them. But that will not happen as long as you continue to hold onto your attachment to feeling their disapproval. From everything you have told me, that disapproval isn't even for real; they are trying to contact you, apparently because they want you back in their lives. But you are refusing to accept what they may have to offer because an unconscious part of you is holding on for dear life to that attachment to rejection and disapproval."

"I feel I have a right to be angry at them," Blake said.

"Yes, you do feel that way. But that feeling is part of your defense. As long as you feel justified in your anger, you are secretly holding onto and indulging in rejection and disapproval. Then you will only defeat yourself. You will remain mired in a victim mentality, and you will stoke the fires of your own negativity."

"I'm here and I'm willing to look at this and change it. Just tell me how to do it."

"You need to see your complicity, your own involvement, in your continuing anger, your depressions, and self-hatred. You want to see your dark side, with its self-defeating agenda, hidden in your unconscious. An aspect of that involves seeing and understanding that a part of you wants to remain a victim of your parents and their neglect and alleged neglect of you. This is what you want to learn about yourself. You appear quite capable of learning this and benefiting greatly from it."

This following exercise offers an opportunity for readers to look into their "grudge drawer" for understanding of their own attachments to rejection.

List all the "crimes" you feel others have perpetrated against you. For each, answer the following:

a) How did you feel? Example, "My wife had an affair. I felt betrayed, unloved, abandoned, rejected, etc."

b) How did you react? Example, "I got mad and never wanted to see my wife again. I withdrew from her and punished her by rejecting her."

c) Is there a pattern where you respond in this manner to those who you feel hurt you? Example, "Yes, when people hurt or reject me, I withdraw and cut them out of my life."

d) Recall an example from your childhood when a similar situation occurred and you felt the same way. Example, "I remember when I got in trouble at school, my mother betrayed me by believing the other kid instead of me, and she punished me unjustly."

e) What could you have done in each case to have avoided this situation or avoided making it worse for yourself? Example, "I could have paid more attention to the relationship between my wife and myself, and what was going on between us. We needed more communication about our problems, rather than having me dismiss them."

f) Consider whether you are doing anything that subtly

provokes rejection. Example, "Yes, I recall that my tone of voice and facial expressions were often critical and judgmental of her."

g) Consider a possible alternate explanation for your prolonged suffering involving each rejection experience. Try to feel or intuit what is going on beneath the surface. Example, "Since rejection is such a theme in my life, could it be that I am secretly looking for the feeling of being betrayed and rejected?"

Many addictive personalities are plagued by their secret willingness to wallow in rejection and disapproval. They are quick to see, hear, or imagine themselves the objects of dislike, criticism, and scorn. Unconsciously, they will plunge into these feelings and be reluctant to come out of them. As their awareness of the nature and extent of their attachment to rejection grows, freedom from addictions and compulsions is won.

Chapter 10

Compulsions Galore

Compulsions come in all sizes and shapes, and some are more self-defeating or self-damaging than others.

Compulsive shoppers go searching for merchandise when it is really happiness they wish to buy. All they manage to buy is time—a brief respite from negative emotions gnawing in the gut.

Often they do not even use the items they buy. One client, Joyce, gave away to family and friends bundles of clothes with price-tags still on. Her husband was a millionaire who give her $50,000 a year in personal spending money, but she resented him for not "taking care of me adequately."

Every time Joyce felt denied, especially in some dispute with her husband, she felt righteous indignation and went on a spending spree. Her defense mechanism would, in effect, exclaim: "You think I like being denied by you, you creep! You see, I'm going out right now to buy anything I want, and you can't stop me."

Joyce ran up enormous credit-card bills and, with her other extravagances, could not manage the debt. She asked her husband to pay it off. When he refused, she went out on another wild spending spree. She told him, "I wouldn't be in this difficult position if you had taken care of me properly in the first place."

The unconscious dynamics are often similar for the compulsive shopper and for the compulsive overeater. The compulsive activity is a reaction to (and also a defense against) secret attachments to deprivation, control, and rejection. People who "shop-til-they-drop" often spend more than they can afford and end up in financial difficulty. Despite this self-damage, they are compelled (through the defense mechanisms) to cover up their secret attachments. So they stagger home with armloads of merchandise that serve as "proof" that they are not passively indulging in feeling deprived but that they really want to get. A day or two later, however, the merchandise no longer compensates for the inner emptiness, and the cycle of dissatisfaction returns.

Attachments to the feelings of rejection are common among compulsive shoppers. When such a shopper feels rejected by a spouse or lover, he will brood over feeling rejected. To compensate and to try to raise his spirits, he will go on a shopping binge. In the shopping, he is "giving" to himself, "caring" for himself, covering up or compensating for his indulgence in rejection. The shopping excursion provides only temporary relief for his emotional distress. It is a very expensive psychic pain-killer.

A variation on compulsive shopping is compulsive shoplifting. Hundreds of thousands of shoplifters are caught and prosecuted each year, and many of these people steal for emotional reasons, not because they are hungry or poor. Often these are people who experienced shame and humiliation for their allegedly bad or naughty behaviors in their childhoods. These individuals remain attached to feelings of being caught and punished, and exposed as "bad," and they choose some forbidden activity such as shoplifting to flirt with these feelings. They do not have to be caught in shoplifting to play this dangerous game. They can simply imagine themselves being caught and punished and feel again the old shame and humiliation that is carried from their past and recreated when they reproach and condemn themselves for their bad behavior.

The school-yard bully offers a good example of how a compulsion works. Studies have shown bullies are frequently children who are being abused verbally or physically in their home by neurotic parents. The youngster passively endures this abuse and unconsciously becomes attached to it. He then goes to school and defends against his passive attachment to being the victim by identifying with the abusive parent. His defense proclaims, "I'm not passively attached to being criticized and abused by my father. If anything, I'm the aggressor." Now he finds some smaller child in the school yard and beats up on him. What is even more devious is that he now identifies with the person he is picking on, and in this way again he re-experiences his attachments to being victimized.

One client, who was struggling to reform his excessive consumption of food and alcohol, had been raised by a mother who was verbally abusive. Now, as an adult, he had a tendency to "badmouth" others, especially in front of the employees of his business establishment where he would berate the character flaws of certain customers. He often felt hostility arise when certain types of potential customers entered his store. Despite his best intentions to sell them merchandise, he could not entirely conceal his negative thoughts and feelings toward them, and he knew this cost him a lot of business. Yet he was compelled to be judgmental and disapproving of them. His aggressive behavior toward them was a defense against his own passive attachment to feelings of disapproval coming at him, starting in his own childhood.

A person can be compulsive about completing all the tasks on his list. One client was extremely competent and responsible and worked as a manager in a business. Because she was so organized and conscientious, her boss kept loading her with more and more work. She became desperate because the work load was so heavy, yet she felt compelled to complete everything that was assigned.

Consciously, she felt the need to please everyone, especially her boss. Unconsciously, however, she was attached to the feeling of being disapproved of.

Her defense against this attachment to disapproval was to be a "people pleaser" and do everything assigned no matter how much stress and anxiety it caused, in order to "prove" how much she disliked the disapproval to which she was secretly attached.

Addictive personalities have great resistance to facing themselves and taking responsibility for what is happening in their lives. They often convince themselves their problems are something other than what they really are. They reinvent reality to preserve the illusion that they are "all-together."

Blaming, for instance, is a common way of restructuring reality to save face and avoid recognition of one's self-suffering. An addictive personality is often emotionally convinced that his troubles are the fault of others. He will blame others and avoid seeing how his own inner feelings and beliefs contribute to his troubles.

Consider the compulsive gambler. The gambler is secretly attached to the feeling of losing. His major defense, however, is to rush to the telephone to call in a bet to his bookie to "prove" that he really wants to win. His gambling is out of control to the degree that he is attached to losing. He becomes convinced that his compulsion is due to a lack of willpower, or selfishness, or cruelty to his wife, or being a bad father, or being too lazy to make an honest living. He will not be aware of the real cause of his compulsion–his attachment to the feeling of losing. Told this, he will usually resist believing it or even considering it.

Another client, in her mid-thirties, was a compulsive exerciser. Despite her attractive figure, she was frantic that she weighed five pounds more than she had in her early twenties. She worked out religiously in a health spa but failed over a year to lose the five pounds. "I hate to look at myself in the mirror," she said. This woman had an attachment to the feeling of being disapproved of. She had experienced substantial parental disapproval in her childhood. Now, in worrying frantically about how she looked, she was unconsciously indulging in her attachment to disapproval, a strong holdover from her childhood experience. She became like her parents to herself and subjected herself to daily critical evaluations. To cover up her attachment to disapproval, she needed desperately "to look good," and so she became compulsive in her exercising.

Another client, Ruth, was compulsive about cleaning. She became distressed and anxious whenever she saw her home in the least bit of disorder. Her alcoholic mother had been highly neurotic, with extremely low self-esteem, and had engaged in housecleaning binges in the middle of the night.

Ruth had two issues with her compulsion. First, she identified with her house and its cleanliness as her mother had. In her unconscious she would indulge in feeling disapproval whenever she could imagine (or see in reality) that people were disapproving of her house or its lack of cleanliness. Her attachment was to feeling disapproval, and the compulsive cleaning was a defense: "I'm not looking to be disapproved of–see how nice I want my house to look so people will think well of me."

Second, Ruth had in her childhood felt controlled and manipulated by her parents. Both parents had been alcoholics, and they had required her to be extra responsible to compensate for their frequent lapses. As an adolescent she did all the housecleaning and hated having to do it. Now her parents were dead, but her childhood experience had conditioned her to go on unconsciously looking for the feeling of being controlled. This passivity was the feeling she succumbed to when she felt compelled to clean house.

Another client, Tom, compulsively watched TV every night, sitting in a semi-stupor for hours. At his job as an accountant, Tom felt controlled and harassed by his supervisors. He complained about how they failed to appreciate his hard-working efforts. He felt his wife nagged at him, protested that he did not make enough money, and compared him unfavorably to her sister's husband, all of which added to his store of inner resentments. He said he did not get from his wife, that she was sexually cold toward him, and offered no support or appreciation. Tom's inclination was to avoid her and shut her out and substitute TV for intimacy. Shutting her out, and thereby cutting himself off as well from intimacy, was a manifestation of his attachment to being emotionally deprived and unrecognized. His attachment to these feelings impeded him from reforming his situation.

Compulsive sex or sex addiction also indicates an unconscious attachment to rejection and emotional deprivation. To cover up this secret attachment, the compulsive individual feels a conscious need for being loved, wanted, validated, and being number one in the other person's life. This person is so desperate for "love" that he convinces himself that sex is love.

One woman felt a compulsion to have sex as soon as possible in relationships. She displayed no ability to say no to sexual advances. This woman had a difficult time supporting herself financially and was aware of wanting someone to support her. In fact, she was acting out her childhood fear, which had become her secret attachments: feelings of being unloved and abandoned. As a youngster, the only time her father had shown her the least interest was when he molested her. She associated sex with the feeling of being wanted and taken care of. Now as an adult, sex became a kind of drug that created an illusion of love. But the day after her sexual encounters, she was back to feeling unloved, unwanted, rejected.

For such people, sex is a substitute for the breast. Missing daily sex feels like starving emotionally. No sex feels like "no love." When sex is missed, a conscious feeling of anxiety and sometimes fear arises. If the partner refuses sex, for whatever reason, the refusal is taken as rejection.

Compulsive sex is a defense that provides "evidence" that the individual wants to be loved. Deep down though is the secret attachment to feeling unloved. The defense goes like this: "But I do want to be loved, see how desperate I am for their love. I take it any way I can get it." If the individual is not willing to explore the anxiety and see where it is coming from, he will have less chance to reform his compulsive behavior. This person will be compulsive and act out sexually to the degree that he or she is attached to feeling rejected or unloved.

Compulsive sex may be the escape of choice, rather than alcohol or drugs. One woman said of her boyfriend, "I don't know what to do. He never gets enough sex. I'm worn out trying to service him." This man was trying to release his stress and emotional conflicts through sex. When he got upset with his business partner, he would come home and want sex three or four times to deal with his emotional reactions from work. If she refused him, he would masturbate. In this case, several attachments were behind his compulsion–feeling controlled, taken advantage of, rejected, refused.

Masturbation is sometimes compulsive, out of control. One client remembered how, as a teenager, he masturbated every night despite his wish not to do so and despite the guilt and anxiety this behavior provoked in him. Often he would be imagining his mother bursting in on him, catching him in the act. His mother was controlling and prudish, and he imagined her stricken with horror had she ever caught him. However, he left tell-tale signs of his activity, such as stains on the floor and in his underwear, and realized later she could not have failed to have known. In his mind, his mother judged him critically, had little faith in him, and expected the worst from him. His compulsion was fueled by his attachment to the feelings of being caught, condemned, and punished. And he was compelled to act out in a manner that instigated these feelings.

Generally, compulsive masturbation is a result of underlying feelings of being refused and rejected. The compulsion therefore represents *a giving to oneself* of love and pleasure.

Another client, George, had been a male prostitute and drug user in his teens. He felt his father had rejected him in childhood. "I wasn't the son he wanted," George recalled. "I can remember frequent looks of disgust from him at the dinner table, just for little things I did. He made me feel I was bad, even terrible."

Once his father hauled George down to a police station and tried to have him jailed for misbehaving; the police refused since he had not broken any law. George's older sister was also scornful of him, and he became a target of her anger and disgust. Another time his father, who was unfaithful to George's mother and eventually divorced her, brought home a briefcase containing hard-core pornography. George got into this material while his parents were out and was harshly punished after being caught reading it and masturbating when his parents returned unexpectedly.

"If my father was going to look at me with disgust, I was really going to show him something to be disgusted about," George said of his drug use and promiscuity.

George's compulsion to be "naughty" was based on his attachment to the feelings of being scorned, rejected, and condemned. George defended against his attachments by offering this rationale: "I'm not passively attached to being scorned and rejected. On the contrary, the problem is I really am a bad character and deserve the scorn and rejection I get. In other words, I actively bring it on myself." In feeling that he was bad, George pleaded guilty to a supposed lesser crime (being bad) to cover up what his unconscious deemed to be the greater crime, his passive indulgence in feeling rejected and condemned. In this way, he claimed power: "I, by being bad, cause the condemnation." Believing this about himself, he found it easy to act out being bad (becoming a male prostitute).

Once a person engages in this type of defense, he will be caught up in guilt, shame, and the conviction of his own worthlessness, as he continues to feel compelled to be bad.

Harvey, a man in his fifties, was out of control in terms of his desire to pursue women and was compulsive in his extramarital activities. He had lost count of his affairs and one-night stands in a fifteen-year stretch during his marriage. When he came to therapy he had been married to the same woman for almost twenty-five years and was involved in a three-year affair with a younger woman.

The younger woman was urging Harvey to divorce his wife and marry her, and indicated she would not wait much longer for him to decide. Harvey was in agony. He feared making a wrong decision. He said he still cared about his wife, although he had not had sex with her for six months. His wife, he said, would be devastated if he left her. However, he really wanted the other woman. Sex was great with her, he said, and she was devoted to him.

"What am I going to do?" he asked desperately. "The problem is, I don't even have an inkling which woman to choose. I wish I could be married to both. I'm very insecure about choosing one or the other."

Harvey's ambivalence was caused by his attachment to loss or the feeling of missing out. Whatever choice he considered brought about the prospect of missing out on the other woman. He was sitting on the fence, paralyzed by the feeling of impending loss. He did not see making a choice or commitment as a gain but as a loss to mourn.

At the end of his first session, he became agitated about whether or not he dared risk filling health claims for psychological services, fearing his use of such services would become gossip at his company.

"That's so unfair!" he protested. "I pay more than $2,000 a year for this insurance." In that moment, he had gone straight into another encounter with the feeling of loss.

"Okay, I see that I'm doing this indulging," Harvey told me. "Now what? Is that the answer? Do I just see it? How does it get better?"

"Once you see and understand a secret attachment," I said, "it will begin to go away. You are learning something deep and profound about yourself, and that learning empowers you as you feel and integrate this new awareness. Seeing patterns of misunderstanding and self-defeat, both in the past and in the present, is part of the learning process. The learning occurs not just intellectually but on a feeling and intuitive level.

"The main thing is to watch your reactions objectively and to define what you feel. Ask yourself, 'Where is this feeling coming from?' You will find yourself beginning to see and consider more appropriate choices in how to react or behave in situations. It is this ongoing process of exposing the operations of self-suffering that finally reforms your character and ends the suffering."

Some people are emotionally addicted to pornography and become compulsive peepers of sexual images. The primary problem with this compulsion involves feelings of worthlessness. The more worthless a person feels, the more he will be attracted to images of people who, in their flagrant sexual exhibitionism, also appear to be exhibiting a sense of worthlessness. This is because he can take comfort and defend against the inner alignment with feelings of worthlessness by claiming, "At least I am not as worthless as these people obviously are." Meanwhile, he is "turned on" through his identification with the models' wanton indifference toward dignity and self-respect.

Those who protest most loudly against pornography, claiming it degrades women, also have issues with worthlessness. They are identifying with the degraded models, while covering up (or defending against) their attachments to worthlessness through their protests ("See how much I hate pornography. I'm not looking to identify with these models and their expressions of worthlessness"). Both the compulsive peepers and the loudest protesters are encumbered by inner attachments to feelings of worthlessness.

Other types of compulsions revolve around money and possessions. One client, Thomas, had a million dollars to invest. He was unable to tolerate the feeling of having those funds earn only six percent in safe investments when he saw others making ten percent on their riskier investments. So he gambled and lost $100,000 in a speculative scheme. He came to therapy depressed after this ill-conceived gamble with a crooked partner.

Thomas remembered as a child watching his parents locked in vicious verbal battles that terrorized him. Fear, helplessness, and convictions of abandonment overwhelmed him during these fights. He developed deep expectations of being without emotional support, which he compensated for as an adult by projecting security onto money.

Asked what he feared the most, Thomas said losing all his money, becoming destitute, being without a home, on the street, and abandoned. Thomas was very successful and his fears of ending up on the Bowery were highly unfounded. His obsession with money was a defense to cover up feelings from childhood of helplessness and abandonment. No one would abandon him if he were rich. The neediness that prompted him to pursue money compulsively was self-defeating because his inner conflict kept him from being happy no matter how much money he had.

Often he felt guilty, so he decided his problem was excessive greed. Thomas may have been acting greedily for all to see, but greed was a secondary issue. He became more secure as he understood that his greed was a consequence of his secret attachments to feelings of deprivation and abandonment. The greed served as a defense to establish that he really wanted to get and be secure, similar to how a compulsive shopper compensates for attachments to deprivation, control, or rejection.

A variation of the greedy person is the compulsive miser. The miser believes, ironically, that of his own free will he has chosen a way of life that brings him pleasure. In fact his way of life is forced on him by a specific defense in the unconscious. The miser is a bundle of fears, compulsions, and obsessions centered around money. What the miser calls his pleasures are really desperate inner attempts to alleviate the misery of being a miser.

The miser is consumed with the idea of being taken advantage of. To establish that he does not unconsciously enjoy the idea of being hoodwinked, he "proves" through his miserly behavior that he really wants to keep what he has. He is also absorbed with the idea of outsmarting others, but he ends up outsmarting himself through his inability to enjoy leisure and luxury. He can not enjoy himself when he is thinking about the amount of money it is costing or the prospect of losing it.

Of course, it is often wise to be frugal, but a penny-pinching mentality can keep a person from even enjoying going out to dinner. He will complain about the cost of a head of lettuce or the charges for long-distance phone calls. He is always evaluating how much he is spending, which means emotionally he is attached to the feeling of how much he is being drained or how much he is losing.

Another variety of money compulsion involves people who give away or loan out funds that they can ill afford to spend or lose. One woman had been dating a man for five months when he asked her for a $5,000 loan to help him start a new business. She agreed to this without asking for a written contract. Shortly after, they fought and broke up, and she could not get her money back. This was not the first time she had loaned to others and not gotten it back. The woman was acting out a secret attachment to the feeling of losing and being taken advantage of.

Another woman could not say *no* to friends and relatives who asked her for money for whatever reason. Although she herself was struggling to pay her own bills, she gave freely from her limited funds. Through this behavior she perpetuated her own deprivation, then she would moan and groan and complain that she was never appreciated and never got in life.

In another case, a businessman was a frequent sucker for con men and get-rich scams. He had a pattern of being taken advantage of, especially by business partners, and was acting out an expectation of losing and being betrayed.

Some people are compulsively punctual. If you are this way and are late for some scheduled event, you would be anxious, even panicky. Behind this compulsion are three primary attachments. One is the emotional conviction that you will miss out and be deprived by being late. The second is the conviction that you will be disliked and rejected for having kept someone waiting. Third is the fear of inner voices of reproach or condemnation for "not doing what's expected," or "what you're supposed to do," or for "messing up" in the conduct of your life.

In contrast, some people are chronically late for appointments or work. Here the primary attachment is to the feeling of being forced or compelled to follow some imposed schedule or timetable. Being late becomes the passive-aggressive reaction (defense) against the feeling of being controlled or forced: "No one forces me–I come and go as I please."

One's attitude to time can be used as a defense to cover up an attachment to deprivation. A preoccupation with time blocks out the experience of getting. Anxiety levels are elevated by convictions that there is never enough time, time is money, or time is running out. Many people experience time as a drain down which pours their energy, wealth, health, and status. Time is absolute, not relative, for those who use it to measure loss and deprivation.

Fast driving also can be compulsive. This happens when people become provoked and emotional behind the wheel of a car. Distressed by the feeling of being held up by other drivers, they compensate for this feeling by speeding and cutting in and out of traffic. One client with this compulsion had many tickets and several near-accidents. In therapy, he revealed that he did not walk until he was two years old because his mother, afraid he would fall and hurt himself, always took his hand and *held him up*. In another instance, he was tormented when an academic program of his was held up by teachers for repeated revisions. Although he was not a problem drinker, he found himself more inclined to drink when frustrated and anxious in feeling delayed or held up.

Another client, Sam, was a fast-paced, heavy-drinking businessman. He suffered emotionally when his partners were slow in developing their projects. Sam took their slower pace emotionally, feeling they were holding him up personally rather than understanding that they just were not able or inclined to work at his speed. A keen golfer, he would not enjoy his sport when being held up, even for a few minutes, by players in front. So on weekends he got to the golf course at the crack of dawn to be first off the tee.

When Sam was in elementary school, his twin brother had been ill and missed classes for most of one year. His parents decided to keep both boys back one year in the same grade rather than have Sam proceed ahead without his brother. Now, with his unconscious attachment to the feeling of being held up, the danger was for Sam to compensate (defend) by becoming urgent about business decisions and resentful toward his partners for allegedly holding him up. The consequence was unnecessary frustration and the prospect of making rash decisions.

The workaholic is another compulsive. The person who nearly destroys himself with overwork is often regarded more worthy than those who seek more balance and harmony in their lives. But the workaholic is as dependent on work as the addict on his drug. Often the workaholic is secretly attached to being a violated passive victim of some greater power (parents, bosses, company, social expectations, recognition), which has total control and determines his fate. "No, not true that I'm passive and want to be a slave to others," his unconscious defends, "I'm just working hard, which is doing what Mom and Dad taught me and what everyone says is good."

Many workaholics had parents who based self-worth solely on success and accomplishment, particularly to mask their own low self-esteem. The problem for the workaholic is that he applies what he was taught like a weapon of self-torture.

This method of defense is called a *pseudo-moral.* The person takes some decent moral lesson from his parents or society and reduces the lesson to absurdity by misusing it to serve as a psychological defense. The lesson, "It is good to work hard" becomes the defense, "Look how innocent I am of passivity, of wanting to feel deprived or forced. See how aggressively I drive myself with work."

The workaholic is not comfortable being liked for who he is, so the focus is put on what he can do. Money, success, and power are pursued to "prove" that he really does want to get, that he does want to be in control of his life. As long as workaholics fail to understand their passivity, they will remain driven to acquiring objects, praise, and promotions. This inner compulsion is completely different from the healthy worker who labors out of choice and pleasure, and who enjoys work for its opportunities to prosper, to be of value to others, and to be creative.

The workaholic feels chronically dissatisfied and let down by his own efforts or by the efforts of others. Usually without being aware of it, workaholics have a punitive, scolding attitude toward themselves. Their self-depreciation not only occurs at times of failure, but is an on-going emotional experience that undermines self-satisfaction even when things are going well.

Rachel, a workaholic, had been tormenting herself for several days about five bags of mulch laying in her yard. Although she was working twelve-hour days at her job, and needed to rest during her off hours, she felt distressed that she had not yet spread the bags of mulch in her flower garden. The bags produced, she said, "the feeling of not having accomplished anything."

She had a difficult time enjoying leisure. "I always feel there is something I should be doing. I feel I waste time if I'm not accomplishing something."

As a child, Rachel remembered the chronic feeling of not doing well enough and that both parents judged her on the basis of her performance. "I always felt pressure, especially to get good marks in school," she said, "I felt I didn't excel as I should have. Even though I was on the honor roll every year, Mom made me feel it was still not good enough."

Rachel felt emotional turmoil over a C she received in a

college math course and could not bring herself to tell her parents. Her parents had both been dissatisfied with their own accomplishments in life and, in their constant focus on the daughter's performance, projected their own expectations of failure onto their daughter.

Rachel said her father, an engineer, was reserved and quiet, and never spoke much about his expectations for his children. "But we all knew what he wanted–four intellectuals." Her father was annoyed when she switched her major from mathematics to history while in college.

Rachel's major issue was her attachment to feeling disapproval. Even though her father did indeed appear to have disapproved of her, she learned she did not have to carry around her sensitivity to that feeling once she saw her secret role in maintaining it. In her job as a manager, she had been compulsive about performance because she felt she would be judged critically if anything went wrong, even in areas beyond her control. She had identified with her place of work and taken any criticism of it personally. With insight, she began to free herself from those feelings that had haunted her from her past.

Rachel's fear of disapproval reflected her expectation of getting it. When no one was around to disapprove of her, she would disapprove of herself, as she did for not spreading the bags of mulch. As she worked out her attachments to disapproval and emotional deprivation, she also began to free herself from her workaholic tendencies.

Chapter 11

Exposing Secret Attachments

In dealing with addictions and compulsions, many different combinations of secret attachments can come together to create a person's own unique blueprint for self-defeat. As a psychotherapist, I try to penetrate the defense mechanisms to expose an individual's inner combination of attachments. This chapter is an extension of the "Hidden Feelings" chapter and is designed to help readers expose and understand their own secret attachments.

Let us look again into the inner workings of compulsive gamblers and speculators (who often are also substance abusers). On the surface, gamblers and speculators desperately want to win. Unconsciously, however, they expect to lose and are attached to the feeling of losing. This means they are predisposed to seek out and to act out in some manner the experience of losing. Notice that society calls compulsive gamblers *losers.* Losing is their greatest worry, even their greatest fear. But in the unconscious, what you fear in this irrational manner is what you are secretly attached to.

When compulsive gamblers hit a losing streak, they are

absolutely miserable and may react or compensate with substance abuse, other compulsive behaviors, or with obsessions or phobias. Sometimes, of course, they do win, and their "manic highs" on winning become defenses that "prove" that it is winning, not losing, they so desperately seek. The confirmed gambler seldom quits when he is ahead because, at that point, he has not yet received what he came for–fulfillment of the inner attachment to losing. He convinces himself he will win more and more, and becomes willing to risk large sums. Las Vegas owes its diamond-studded glitter to the secret attachment to loss.

The attachment to losing is accompanied by the gambler's thrill of uncertainty–a manic excitement or powerful tension associated with the game–that even overshadows his greed for money. The greater the risk, the greater the tension. This tension is caused by the gambler's masochistic flirtation with the feeling of being "naughty" and the prospect of impending punishment in the form of reproach from others (or self-reproach) for the unconsciously anticipated losses.

Meanwhile, on the surface, the gambler displays a pathological optimism in his conviction that he will win. He is aware of his inner rebellion against morals, moderation, and other educational rules given by society (originally mother and father)–but he is not aware this rebellion is a self-defeating reaction to his lingering, substantial megalomania.

Like the gambler, the speculator is taking on society and educational rules that state that normal conduct consists in working hard and making a contribution to life. He is predisposed to defy the educational commands because they aim to undermine his precious infantile belief that he can do whatever he pleases. The speculator comes armed with his rationalizations (defenses): "Look at the millions of dollars others are making in the stock market and in futures trading. People are getting rich without working. Why should I be a sucker and work hard all my life?"

On the surface, it looks as if the speculator is desperate to get. But he is more likely to lose. As a child, he was emotionally stabilized at the deprivation level. Now he is setting up a drama to act out once again his self-damaging pattern. Sometimes when he is ahead on the stock or futures markets, a part of him will be reluctant to cash in his winnings. His inner urge is to tempt fate—and let the pot ride. Often, he will invoke magical thinking (remnants of megalomania) that induces him to be superstitious or to believe he is destined to win on a grand scale.

In compulsive gambling and speculating, the risk of loss is enormous. We see how these people become (losers) what they are attached to (loss). Another compulsive type is the perfectionist. He too becomes (a critic or judge, often of himself) what he is attached to (being criticized). The perfectionist is quick to reproach himself anytime he does some little thing wrong. His is a lose-lose proposition because he is always looking for what is imperfect in himself or his work and feeling judged for his imperfections. As an ideal, perfectionism can help individuals do splendid work. But as a personality quirk that serves as a psychological defense, it will drive a person to exasperation.

The perfectionist is trapped inside a mentality that harbors the conviction that others will be critical and judgmental of him. From this perspective, the planet is populated only by critics, judges, evaluators, assessors, and graders. Again, his problem is a secret attachment to the feeling of these critics looking over his shoulder at "imperfections" in his work, personality, or attributes.

In one instance, a client got caught between two secret attachments, feeling controlled and feeling criticized. Gloria, a perfectionist, had returned with a massive headache after a day-long bus excursion with her women's club members.

On the trip she sat beside a talkative woman and felt helpless, forced to talk and listen to this woman for hours. When Gloria considered ignoring the woman and reading a book or trying to sleep, she began to imagine that this woman would be displeased with her and consider her rude, which played into my client's attachment to being criticized.

"You could have been pleasant to this woman for a while, and then told her you have to rest, that you're not feeling well," I told Gloria. "Since your predicament made you anxious, that certainly wouldn't be a lie. But that's only advice. It's insight that will help you more because then you will have your own answers and solutions.

"You know the issues in this instance," I continued. "They are your attachments to feeling controlled and to feeling criticized. And you can see how you're caught in the middle of them. When you asserted yourself and ignored the woman, you became entangled in feeling guilty, caused by the fact you were secretly indulging in feeling criticized by her. When you continued to talk and listen to her, you became angry and frustrated and developed a headache as a consequence of secretly indulging in feeling controlled and helpless.

"To deal with your predicament, try to observe these attachments in operation. As you do that, your appropriate behavioral response to deal with this kind of challenging situation will come to you."

Gloria had another unconscious difficulty in this situation. She was convinced the other woman would feel less than, unimportant, or demeaned if she ignored her. This is precisely what Gloria would feel if someone appeared to be ignoring her. So Gloria imagined that the woman was experiencing those feelings and identified with her. Gloria then became anxious as she felt her unhappiness in the woman's company because she was indulging (vicariously, through the woman) in the feeling of being unimportant or less than. The realization that she was involved in this attachment was another key to alleviating her guilt and anxiety.

Gloria's secret attachments in her present life corresponded with the circumstances and experiences of her childhood. Her mother had been passive, out of touch with her own needs and feelings and those of her daughter, and subservient to Gloria's father. Gloria had become like her mother and had little capacity to feel and exhibit her own value. She took on her mother's attachments to feeling less than, inadequate, and unworthy. Her father had showed little emotional interest in Gloria or her mother. Gloria had taken personally this apparent rejection, believing that his lack of interest was due to faults of her own, and so she became more convinced of her inadequacy. Meanwhile, her father was extremely sensitive to being disapproved of or criticized, and Gloria had acquired these attachments from him.

As mentioned, a characteristic of many addictive personalities is their preoccupation with being judged as bad and deemed unworthy. Remember what it was like to come home with a report card, to feel the apprehension of being judged, to tremble at the prospect of being considered inadequate or mediocre. Children wait breathlessly for that look on their parents' faces—the frown, the disappointment, the scowl. "What about this B? How come it's not an A? What happened to you in Math? Why can't you get good grades like your sister?"

Inside himself, the youngster may feel unworthy, disliked, stupid, or condemned. Judgment scenarios are repeated thousands of times in childhood, only to continue relentlessly in one's adult life. When guests arrive for dinner, it is Judgment Day. When it is time to give a speech to colleagues, it is Judgment Day. Every day is Judgment Day in some fashion or other. People are always judging each other for their clothes, cars, homes, physical features, brains, bank accounts, and hair-cuts. An arrogant personality is one defense used against the attachment to being judged and looked down on.

Defensiveness is a sure sign of secret attachments. "Why do you go on the defensive so easily?" I asked one client who was feeling criticized by his wife. "Is there anything you really have to defend against? This defensive mode of yours is the problem in itself. It means you are desperate to cover up your attachment to feeling criticized, and so you energetically defend against the feeling of being criticized, vehemently protesting your innocence of wrongdoing. The degree to which you go on the defensive reveals how much of an issue you have with feeling accused and being seen as inadequate. Normally, the only defending someone has to do is in a court of law. Sometimes, of course, we have to *explain* our actions. But, unlike defensiveness, the process of explaining is done with little or no emotional distress."

One client, a compulsive overeater, could not drive down the street without looking around herself thinking and feeling that other drivers perceived her as perfectly *in*capable of driving correctly. Consequently, she put great effort into driving perfectly, at the "right" speed, in the "correct" lane. Nonetheless, she continued to watch in the rear-view mirror and in the cars alongside her for anticipated frowns of disapproval in the faces of drivers and passengers.

Another client, a problem drinker, felt anxious when he sat in the front row at school or in church. Secretly, he harbored the conviction that all eyes were on him, disapproving of him for any conceivable reason. Even if no one noticed him sitting in the front row, he would imagine that they were not only noticing him but also being critical. He was likely to behave inappropriately in front of others and then claim (as a defense) that people looked at him because he did silly or outrageous things.

Feeling worthless is a major problem for addictive personalities. The feeling is a result of secret attachments to feeling criticized, disapproved of, disliked, betrayed, or rejected. A compulsive overeater said in a session, "I don't care if I lose weight. What's the use? Why should I bother with this struggle? It's easier to give in." She expressed these sentiments because she had slipped into feeling worthless.

"Next time you feel the urge to eat at the wrong time," I told her, "take five minutes before you do it and repeat to yourself, over and over, trying to sense its truth: 'Look how I am being drawn into another encounter with feeling disapproved of, disliked, and rejected. This must be what I really want! I really get off on the feeling of being rejected or seen by others as less than.'

"This is a kind of reverse psychology that confronts the source of your inner conflict. This reverse psychology is intended to overcome the problems of denial and repression. You have to see what you're doing. You can't fix a car or a computer unless you know what's wrong with it. In the unconscious, you only have to *see what you're doing that is self-defeating* and want to fix it, and improvement will happen."

For dramatic effect, I provided metaphors for her predicament: "It's as if you're a baby eagerly willing to suck on the breast of rejection, still unwilling after all these years to wean yourself from it. Or you can imagine that, when you overeat, you are feeding that inner demon that is your attachment to feeling less than. You can also look at it this way: your indulgence in feeling unloved creates a kind of emotional vacuum, a great inner emptiness that becomes so profound that you feel compelled to fill up with food."

If a child felt belittled or bad for not being able to satisfy parents' expectations, the child grows up belittling himself and his own efforts, repeating the feeling of looking bad and not being liked or accepted. The individual is now "hooked" on the feeling of being a defective human being who experiences criticism and rejection because "I cause it to happen."

He takes power (an aspect of megalomania) over the rejection by claiming, "It is I who did not try hard enough, and messed up, causing this rejection from my parents." With this defense, he embarks upon endless self-reproach.

As an adult, he has identified with the critical parent in his past and now has become the parent to himself. He now tends to look down upon others and to become the aggressor who criticizes rather than the victim who is passively being criticized. This is a cover-up for his passivity, his willingness to indulge in feeling criticized.

The child, and later the adult, is unconsciously holding onto feeling disapproved of and put down. He cannot give himself a feeling of satisfaction, not having cultivated satisfaction with himself as a child. He will not see or appreciate his successes. In the drive to excel, he will focus on what has not been (or cannot be) achieved. This individual seeks and expects disapproval in much of what he does.

Sometimes clients will criticize themselves for not progressing fast enough in therapy. But everyone progresses at his own pace and there are no quick cures. Though an individual may be doing quite well in therapy, he may decide his recovery is not fast enough and then begin to whip himself for slow progress. I told one client, "Be patient with this process and try not to be so critical of yourself. You are just doing to yourself–being critical–what you expect others to do to you. And your unconscious doesn't care what it uses as material for criticism, so it will even sneak in self-criticism, using your naive supposition that your progress is too slow."

Many authorities believe that a lack of self-esteem causes addictions. It is true that low self-esteem contributes to addictive and compulsive behaviors, but the precise cause and nature of each individual's low self-esteem has to be determined in order to help that person. Low self-esteem is itself a consequence of secret attachments. Once secret attachments are neutralized, self-esteem grows.

The continuation of low self-esteem into adulthood is a result of attachments to feelings of being seen as less than or feeling unloved, criticized, controlled, betrayed, or rejected. People who are *not* worried about how they are being seen or treated by others tend to have a well-developed sense of self.

All people with low self-esteem are preoccupied with how others see them or treat them. They carry the emotional conviction that others see them as somehow inadequate or not good enough. Then they feel bad (low self-esteem) for some alleged deficiency or inadequacy on their part.

For example, mother comes home after a hard day at work, frustrated she did not get a raise, and consequently reacts angrily toward her daughter for not doing the dishes. The daughter takes this personally and feels disapproved of. She feels that her mother does not love her, and she unconsciously holds onto these feelings. The daughter takes it a step further and is convinced that some deficiencies of her own cause her mother to disapprove of her and not like her. Some children interpret events in this self-defeating way, while others maintain a more objective outlook.

"One of the ways to change your low self-esteem," I said to a client, "is to realize how much you are secretly willing to be looked down on and disapproved of by others. This condition causes you to be preoccupied with how you are being seen. Instead of seeing others objectively, you are emotionally involved with your subjective impression of how they are seeing you. The more you understand this, the more you will emerge from self-centeredness into greater objectivity."

Emerging from self-centeredness is part of the growth process. One client could not get a sense of becoming more objective. "Imagine you are an anthropologist," I told him. "You are studying a primitive tribe in the jungle, and you walk about jotting notes for the science article you plan to write. Suddenly, a tribesman rushes up, sticks out his tongue at you and laughs in your face. You do not take this personally, you are not offended or hurt. Perhaps you wonder whether this is a form of salutation. You are fascinated, and you laugh back at your new friend. You have no standards by which to be offended.

"Back in civilization," I continued, "the anthropologist publishes his article. A colleague laughs in his face, claiming some conclusions are preposterous. The anthropologist believes in his work and does not take this challenge personally. He does not identify with the article. If the article is rejected, he may be disappointed, but he does not feel personally rejected. If the colleague's challenge is rude and intended to be personal, the anthropologist deals with that effectively, seeing that his colleague is entangled in some emotional insecurity. This healthy reaction is possible because this anthropologist is not self-centered and is not trapped in self-importance (narcissism or lingering megalomania)."

Many addictive personalities are inwardly terrified that the worthlessness they feel in themselves will be exposed for all to see. Sometimes, to protect themselves, clients try to use their session time reporting on how well they are doing. Unconsciously, they want to prevent the therapist from offering insight or analysis, in part because it feels to them as they hear the analysis that their inadequacy or worthlessness is now confirmed. The insight, of course, is extremely valuable to them; it reveals the origins and nature of their convictions of worthlessness and the means to emerge from it. Nevertheless, the insight can feel like an arrow in the breast as it brings into the open what the client's unconscious is so anxious to cover up—his attachments to feelings of refusal, control, or rejection.

The success hunter is a compulsive runner from feelings of worthlessness. For this individual, it is not enough to make a decent living, support a family and pursue normal social contacts and interests. The urge to get in a spectacular manner becomes a consuming passion for many, and the success hunter has been glorified in movies, magazines, and newspaper stories. Yet healthy individuals are inclined to balance their emotional energy for work with the enjoyment of family life, friends, and leisure activities.

The success hunter's exaggerated ambition represents a defense against feelings of insecurity, low self-worth, loss, and deprivation. The success hunter is contemptuous of the "unsuccessful" because the unsuccessful person provokes in him this inner reproach: "This man is a mirror of yourself, you weakling." To counteract this reproach, the defense of aggressive self-advancement is mobilized, while he feels contemptuous of the weakling.

The success hunter is caught in a deadly spiral of an escalating effort to maintain his defenses. He is unable to relax and enjoy success because an inner fear pushes him on relentlessly. Often, increasingly grandiose plans and maneuvers are needed to ward off the relentless inner reproaches for his attachments to loss of stature and worth. He will tend to be dissatisfied and bored if deprived of new work activities because, in this state of inactivity, he will have to face his insecurity and dissatisfactions.

The success hunter is fond of showing off and is more partial to flattery than is a healthy person. This type must have a continuous diet of flattering approval, his substitute for inner security. Ivan Boesky, one of the major Wall Street players sent to jail in the 1980s for insider trading, had (before he was deposed) written a book glorifying his deals and polishing his self-image. The success hunter's vanity and pompous self-importance thrive on admiration, but he is also aware of the doubters who attribute his success to luck or chance. This skepticism is a great irritant because it reinforces his own inner doubts. The resulting defense is stubbornness and obstinacy.

The success hunter is often without real friends, because such friends are not a source of hypocritical flattery, nor are they ingratiatingly humble. So he works alone, with enormous power to influence the nation's well-being but with his actions increasingly divorced from considerations for the common good. In contrast, the healthy person proceeds with his career on the assumption that it will be fulfilling, rewarding, and enjoyable, and he does not feel the need to run after a jack-pot-in-the-sky.

Millions of people engage in another compulsive behavior that is very subtle—what might be called a secret compulsion. These are *negative peepers* who peer around in their environment and look for what they are not getting; how they are missing out; or how they are being overlooked, criticized, negated, and rejected. With their eyes or their imaginations, they feast on real or imagined scenes to deepen the sense of their own impoverishment or victimization. As a result of the emotional distress produced by this peeping, they often act out with substance abuse or other self-defeating behavior.

A negative peeper focuses on a beautiful woman only to indulge in the feeling of what he is missing in bed rather than to enjoy her beauty. Instead of using his eyes to see beauty and to appreciate life, he uses his eyes to feel deprived. He looks intently into the faces of a group to see which people there are looking back at him with dislike. He takes in all the glamor and sophistication at a party in order to feel less than the others.

Choice in what we see comes early in life. For instance, a six-year-old has lost a shoe. He goes about the house crying, but no one helps him find it. He walks right past the shoe and does not see it. This is because his intent is *not* to find the shoe but to indulge in the feeling that mother is refusing to come to help him find it.

A client, Roberta, recalled a dinner one Sunday evening with her parents and fiance. She enthusiastically shared with them the news that she had signed a new customer on an advertising contract. "That's wonderful, dear," her father replied. Her fiance then shared his good news, that he had been promoted to manager at the retail establishment where he worked. At this, the father jumped up, shook the fiance's hand, greeting the news with intense excitement.

Watching her father, Roberta began to feel disturbed. Suddenly, she felt hurt and resentful. She rose from the table, said she needed to take a walk alone, and left behind her bewildered intimates. Later in her therapy session, it became clear she had indulged at that moment in the feeling that her fiance got more praise and validation than she had. Her negative peeping (seeing her fiance get praise from her father) enabled her to feel unloved and unappreciated. She was triggered by the infantile feeling that if someone else shines, she must be diminished in comparison, a situation she had encountered frequently in childhood when she perceived that her brother was the recipient of more praise and approval than herself.

Her father later revealed that he had not been aware of how important the advertising contract was to her. Rather than belittling her achievement, he had jumped at the news of her fiance's promotion because he wanted him to feel included and accepted by the family. With this understanding, she realized how quick she was to spot opportunities to feel deprived and unrecognized.

Substance abusers frequently engage in negative peeping. The individual visualizes scenes in which his friends or family members are doing something or other to hurt, disparage, or humiliate him. In the extreme, this visual fantasizing produces paranoia.

One compulsive overeater, more than 100 pounds overweight, was terrified of making a presentation to her speech class. Her fear was produced from peeping, in which she imagined the members of her class watching her with critical eyes. She had been observing them give their presentations, always looking for each to be nervous and fail, and being secretly disappointed when each did well.

As she imagined herself giving her paper, she saw her classmates looking critically at her, as she had looked critically at them. It was as if she were putting her own critical eyes into their heads in order to look back judgmentally at herself. Since she was secretly attached to being seen critically, she defended with the feeling, "Oh, I don't want to be seen critically–the problem is that I'm nervous. I do badly and cause them to look at me critically."

She confirmed this analysis when she said, "When I see a good-looking couple, both thin, I hate to look at them. I don't want to see their eyes. I realize now it's because I believe they will be looking at me with scorn or disgust. That must be what I'm secretly looking for."

The addictive personality goes around looking for evidence that he is disliked and will even interpret what he sees to conform with what he secretly wishes to see. Or he can just as easily close his eyes and let his imagination produce improbable fantasies in which he is a victim of the malice of others.

Jennifer, an alcoholic in her forties, had been sober for five years. One summer she travelled to Ohio with her boyfriend, attending a wedding and visiting his family. During the wedding reception, she suddenly felt strongly the temptation to drink alcohol. She had a drink in her hand before she managed to put it down and walk away from it.

What had produced at that moment her powerful impulse to have a drink? Even before embarking on this trip, she had spent days worrying about what to wear, and she had been absorbed in speculation about the impression she would make on her boyfriend's family.

"Once I got there, I was real conscious about being inhibited and holding myself back with those people," Jennifer said in a session. "I feel I didn't have much to say or share with them. Alcohol gave me freedom to act silly, to be outgoing, and to have lots to say to people."

She was anxious and self-conscious at the reception and had felt a drink would relax her and make it easier to participate in the celebration. Although she successfully resisted having a drink, a secret attachment was getting her in trouble. That was her secret willingness to get entangled in feelings of being seen as inadequate or inferior. If she took a drink and became more animated, she would have evidence that she wanted to be seen favorably, to cover up her secret attachment. The impulse to follow through on such a defense can be overpowering, despite the self-damage that might result.

Jennifer could have enjoyed herself at the reception, comfortable with an air of quiet dignity. But she secretly flirted with the negative judgment of her own appearance, and imagined herself being seen as a dizzy blonde with nothing to offer; it was no surprise she was anxious and that she found it difficult to converse easily with others.

She erected her claim-to-power defense: "I'm not attached to being seen negatively. I cause it to happen because I'm not good enough. I'm no longer socially adept. If I could only have a drink, I'd be my old self again." Meanwhile, to show how Jennifer's emotional perceptions clashed with reality, she was approached by many family members who said they liked her and wished her well.

Sometimes we have a compulsion to peep because in childhood we felt visually deprived. Some may recall parental lists of what was forbidden to look at, what we were not supposed to see. One client remembered how her mother became enraged when she discovered her daughter watching a five-year-old male cousin urinating in the toilet. The girl was seriously reprimanded, and since that time she had fantasized about seeing penises, although she could barely bring herself to look at one when opportunities were presented.

As adults, we secretly lust after visual exposure to that which we were forbidden to see–with much guilt attached to the wish. This is an aspect of the appeal of pornography, which some individuals engage in compulsively.

Through his visual drive or emotional imagination, the addictive personality yearns to see evidence that others are against him in some manner. Why would any sensible person, supposedly aligned with his best interests, allow his imagination to torture him in this way? Because he is not in control of this problem. He is overtaken by his conditioning, directed by the unconscious to scan the world–real and imagined–for opportunities to feel rejection, refusal, control, criticism, and humiliation.

Reflection on one's peeping problem helps overcome it. "Reflect on the purpose of your peeping–to feed your attachments to being deprived, controlled or rejected," I told one compulsive overeater who felt "intense pain" whenever he saw or imagined his friends excluding him from their company.

"I imagine them having tons of fun that I'm missing out on," he said. "It's interesting that when I'm with them I'm often bored, but when I'm not there I imagine what I'm missing."

"Just keep at the front of your mind the purpose of your peeping," I said. "The more you develop the realization of the existence of your peeping, and come to accept the way you use it to feed an attachment to rejection, the more you will develop the inner feeling that you can be complete and fulfilled on your own."

Obsessive worriers are a breed of negative peepers. As the worrier looks into the future, he thinks he is trying to prevent bad things from happening. But he is really peeping into the future because his unconscious is wallowing in the feeling of impending disaster, meaning he imagines he is going to miss out, lose out, be controlled, rejected, betrayed, or whatever. Because of these secret attachments, he will have less capacity to enjoy what is happening in the present moment. Instead of using his imagination to enrich his life, he uses it to peer into the future and see only trials, tribulations, and deprivations.

"Your sense of impoverishment is a feeling you are unconsciously willing to cultivate," I told a wealthy client who was peeping into the future, imagining himself impoverished. "In reality, you know you have your funds wisely invested. But you create a new 'reality,' a subjective impression of your future that can only serve one purpose–the promotion of your unhappiness. Only an attachment to deprivation can explain how an intelligent, handsome, and physically healthy person such as yourself can be plagued by such unpleasant feelings concerning your financial well-being."

Mary, an obsessive worrier, had this secret agenda: an attachment to feelings of loss, abandonment, and deprivation. She worried about her family's financial situation, although her husband was a white-collar professional with his own business, and the family was reasonably secure. Mary suffered from chronic boredom and loneliness that indicated the degree to which she indulged in deprivation and feelings of abandonment.

Mary would fantasize gruesome scenes. Once when she was unable to contact her husband by phone because of a busy signal, she imagined he might have died of a heart-attack in the house and left the receiver off the hook. So tormenting was her worry that she called a neighbor to check on him.

Mary's father had been a well-to-do businessman who "lost

everything" during the Depression. "Daddy always said how hard everything was," she remembered. "He hardly ever talked about happy times, only about the bad times."

Mary's parents had fought a lot before finally divorcing when she was a teenager, and she sensed the degree to which she had worried about her security and the outcome of these battles. Once her parents took out a $3,500 mortgage for a house, at an interest rate of four percent and monthly payments of $45. Instead of celebrating on the day the house was purchased, her father sat up all night worrying how to pay back the mortgage.

Mary, who had worried about the prospect of abandonment as long as she could remember, finally realized this fear when her husband of twenty years left her for another woman. Her passivity had contributed to this outcome. Mary had remained naive and dared not challenge him about her suspicions of infidelity, for fear he would leave her. The more she feared abandonment, the more she had become ingratiating and weak, and that had increased the danger her husband would become bored and disenchanted with her. (Of course, her husband also contributed in his own way to their problems.)

Here is a procedure to help identify secret attachments.

A. List what you feel is missing in your life right now. State what you want in specific terms and avoid generalities. Example, "I want more money and a more successful career. Money and success will give me security and a feeling of having. Right now, I feel I don't have enough, and that what I have I'll lose." (This example reveals a secret attachment to missing out, not having, loss.)

B. Write why you want each item on this list. Example, "I'd like a million dollars because then I could do what I want. I would be free, independent and not have to take orders from anyone." (This reveals a secret attachment to feeling controlled, dominated, helpless.)

C. Write out excuses for each item on the list. Why have you not manifested these wishes in your life? Example, "I don't have the necessary assertiveness. My Dad always said I didn't do chores well enough. Now I feel I'm not good enough to go ahead and be successful." (This reveals an attachment to being criticized and seen as inadequate.)

D. Now write how you are responsible for not having what you want in your life. Example, "I take jobs that are beneath my abilities and pay too little." (This reveals an attachment to being seen as inadequate.)

E. Having identified your secret attachments, be alert and watch for them to interfere in your life. Pay special attention to how they interfere with your goals and aspirations. When you are able to spot your secret attachments in action, you have a chance to refrain from becoming entangled in them emotionally and to choose alternative behaviors.

Chapter 12

Flirting With Death

Many individuals go to great lengths, even death, to avoid recognizing their attachments. "I'd rather die than have to face myself and these emotional issues," said a man who never returned for the second session that I had scheduled with him.

One client, Andrew, had a dream that, in the context of his drug problem, illustrated his willingness to flirt with death. He had used marijuana extensively in his twenties and thirties and had then quit for several years. When he was in his mid-forties, he received a present of some strong marijuana and began to smoke it daily. After several weeks, he became aware that the drug, which is a heart stimulant, was causing him some physical discomfort, especially in the heart area. Still, he continued to smoke it, feeling compelled to finish every bit of what he had acquired.

He had a dream in which he was a Confederate soldier who was captured by the enemy and brought into a large hall with other prisoners. The Civil War had just ended, but nevertheless the authorities announced that the prisoners would be executed. Andrew, as the Confederate soldier, stood up and protested, pointing out the injustice and the illegality of this decision. However, he was led into another room and, standing there uncertain of his fate, suddenly turned and looked behind. Andrew saw a Union soldier pointing a rifle at him, and this soldier in blue looked just like himself. In fact, he saw in amazement, the other soldier was himself. Andrew turned and tried to run, but the rifle discharged bringing a piercing pain where the bullet struck him in his back through his heart. He crashed to the floor.

He awoke from this dream with a pain in his heart and sweat on his brow. Later that day he flushed down the toilet the last of his marijuana. Within a few days he was feeling mentally and physically better, quite convinced that an inner enemy, a self-destructive aspect of his unconscious, had been revealed in his dream.

His experience of withdrawal from the marijuana consisted of a nagging sense of loss of the distraction or pleasure offered by the drug. However, because of the potential damage to his health, he believed his consumption of the marijuana represented an unconscious willingness to engage in self-destructive behavior.

A sense of an "enemy within" acting to diminish life also occurred to another client. Patrick had been a wild party-goer in his twenties. He remembered drinking too much many times, being sick in the middle of the night, feeling his heart racing, and saying in the depths of his misery, "This drinking is going to kill me some day." Two years before he started therapy, he had been in a traffic accident in which he had fallen asleep at the wheel and was almost killed. He had also smoked cigarettes but quit during his therapy. He said later he was convinced that cigarette smoking had been another expression of his self-destructive tendencies.

After the accident he had married and pledged to reform his behavior. But he continued drinking heavily. His behavior when he drank began to threaten the marriage. He became sarcastic, cruel, and distrustful toward his wife when he had a few too many drinks. He wanted to stop the drinking completely, but after a few days of abstinence he would feel a powerful urge to celebrate something and have a drink.

"You know," he said, "I don't enjoy the effects of the alcohol like I used to, but I still feel compelled to drink. When I think of stopping, I feel a great loss, like I'll lose something precious."

Patrick felt an emotional desire to reward himself with alcohol and to celebrate. This feeling of deserving a reward or needing to celebrate is often used by addictive personalities to justify their self-destructive behavior. The desire for a reward that is ultimately self-destructive means that the person's alleged good feelings are not firmly grounded by self-respect and self-esteem.

After he had begun to feel at peace with himself, he became aware his addiction to alcohol had involved the following inner pact: "Heavy drinking enables me to avoid looking at the roots of my unhappiness. I focus on my naughty drinking, and thereby avoid looking at underlying emotional issues. As long as I can repress the fact that I am entangled in feelings of being deprived, neglected, and starved emotionally, I accept the consequences of my drinking, the prospect of an early death."

Fred, a businessman in his forties who was abusing his body with too much alcohol and food, feared he would die young. Recently, doctors had told him that his physical condition was precarious, and that his vital organs showed the strain of a man twenty years older. However, he continued to have great difficulty moderating his alcohol and food consumption.

Fred's brother had died suddenly at forty years old. An autopsy failed to pinpoint the cause of death. Both Fred and his brother had been abused as children and had grown up feeling inferior, inadequate, even worthless. Fred remembered how helpless he had felt being beaten several times a week by his father, a large man with huge hands. His brother had not been a substance abuser but had been "raging, angry, pathetic." The brother could only hold odd jobs and often was on welfare. Psychiatrists had determined that he was emotionally impaired.

Fred would frequently awaken in the middle of the night with labored breathing, feeling he was going into a seizure. In those moments, he was convinced emotionally that he was dying. At other times, any chest pain, shortness of breath, or discomfort in the liver or abdomen, caused him to think of death and fear its imminent arrival. Fred fantasized about being alone in a hospital, disabled and helpless, and deserted by his friends and family. This fear of death covered up a secret attachment. The fear served as evidence (a defense) that he was not attached to feelings of rejection, helplessness, abandonment, and worthlessness. His defense contended, "I don't want to feel like my life has no value and that others see me as worthless. Look how much I fear that I might die!" In the ironic twist that is given to all such self-defeating predicaments, his excesses with food and alcohol were hastening his death, the very thing he feared the most.

Paula, a twenty-six-year-old bulimic, revealed her tendency to self-destruction in a variety of ways. She liked doing "risky things," driving fast, climbing rocky ledges. She had recently broken bones in a bad fall on a bicycle that she was racing down a hillside. She had a tremendous fear of being killed by grizzly bears while she lived in Wyoming, an irrational fear which revealed her preoccupation with the prospect of death. In her fears of returning to a bulimic state, food was an enemy that represented death instead of life.

"I call a candy bar 'rat poison,' even while I'm shoving it down my throat," she said.

Drawn to images of emaciation, starvation, and death, she

envied people who were "bony thin" and often wished she had been anorexic instead of bulimic. She had given up on various athletic skills at which she had excelled and gave away many material possessions to friends, She acted out through her attachments to loss and rejection her own unique expression of the death drive.

Judy, a recovered alcoholic in her fifties, recalled the years she had played "Russian roulette" in her self-damaging behavior with alcohol. For twenty years she had flirted with death, drinking to the point at which her addiction produced profound guilt, shame, and medical complications. Then she would pull out to recover and get better for a period of several months before beginning the cycle of self-damage over again. Before she finally quit drinking in her forties, her self-abuse had brought her to the brink of death.

When Judy was a youngster, her father frequently placed her in dangerous situations, which was apparently his way to prepare her to deal with life's challenges. One time he took her out in his boat in gale-force winds in an attempt to teach her to be tough and deal with fear.

"I remember being afraid of my father," she said. "If I didn't do what he wanted, I felt he might destroy me somehow."

For a time in her twenties, she chose police work and had been involved in several potentially dangerous incidents. Following that period, substance abuse became the manner in which she took risks with her life. She was attached to the feeling of helplessly allowing someone or something to do her in. She succumbed to the feeling of being dominated and controlled, and as an adult she created through alcohol the childhood experience of feeling abused, terrorized, and controlled.

The self-destructiveness of defense mechanisms was also revealed in Lisa, a bulimic woman. In her mid-twenties, she was again bingeing and purging shortly after her release from an in-patient program for eating disorders. She had previously been in two other treatment centers and in therapy for four years, and yet felt she had not made any progress with her symptoms in that time. Some nights she would binge and purge five times before finally falling into an exhausted and tormented sleep.

Her father, who was still alive and in his early sixties, had open-heart surgery when he was in his late forties. Five years later he had another open-heart surgery operation. Six years later he had a third heart attack. Lisa remembered that during her childhood her father drank a lot and was also a workaholic. He was very strict, with a fierce temper and disapproving manner. Now, after the heart attacks, he was quiet and soft-spoken, she said.

An exercise instructor, Lisa had begun using amphetamines seven years earlier. She liked the feeling of surging energy and felt this enabled her to lead more dynamic exercise classes. When she could no longer obtain amphetamines, she switched to caffeine tablets and used those for several years. She acknowledged that she was "self-abusive" with these drugs, often taking three or four tablets several times a day. "When I'm abstinent with food, I get very tired and I hate that feeling," she said. "I become overwhelmed by feelings—scared, isolated, angry." She complained of being trapped in "powerful feelings of helplessness."

In her second session, Lisa made this statement: "I'm scared to death of what is happening to me. I'm really afraid I'm going to lose it, meaning my sanity, even my life. I have a great fear of feelings and what's inside, I really do. I feel my disease is going to take me, kill me. It's getting worse and worse. Every time I purge, it's worse."

Lisa was obsessed by the fear of death. Her pronounced fear of death revealed how much she needed to defend against a secret attachment to being controlled, powerless, and helpless to the point of annihilation, as she had felt with her tyrannical father. Lisa was abusing her body with heavy caffeine consumption because the energy boost from the caffeine counteracted her deep sense of passivity and helplessness. This is frequently the appeal behind the use of alcohol and illegal drugs.

Lisa had strong expectations of disapproval. Though her figure was attractive, she was slightly robust and extremely self-conscious about it. She was too embarrassed at times to wear a bathing suit. She continually felt "less than" her friend, a wealthy young woman with a superb figure who was also in recovery. Whenever Lisa did binge and purge, her subsequent self-loathing was very intense.

If Lisa were not a bulimic, her secret attachments would lead her to find another way to experience this harsh self-disapproval. Her addiction to food was a compulsion resulting directly from her emotional addiction to being condemned and punished.

Evidence for this was also provided by one of Lisa's defenses. She "hated it" when she saw others displaying poor table manners, eating with their mouths open. "I have no tolerance for anything," she said. "Little things bother and aggravate me." This reaction revealed how she defended against her own attachments by *condemning* and wanting to *punish* others for a variety of minor transgressions. The more she felt this intense disapproval of others, the more she was compensating for, defending against, and reacting to her own attachment to feelings of being condemned and punished.

When the attachment to the feeling of being condemned and punished is strong enough, an individual's emotional reactions and consequential behaviors become increasingly self-destructive. These aspects are most severe among criminals. The criminal is a self-defeating personality who is caught up in issues of condemnation, social ostracism, and punishment. Criminals, in constant danger of being caught and punished, are acting out their unconscious attachment to these feelings.

Substance abusers also flirt with being caught and punished. Under the law, drug addicts are criminals. They engage in their self-defeating behavior despite the danger to their health *and* despite the prospect of condemnation and punishment.

An alcoholic will often risk driving under the influence despite the prospect of causing an accident and being convicted of manslaughter. The compulsive overeater is attached to the feeling that he will be punished in the form of social ostracism for his obesity. He often sneaks food, anticipating reprimand and punishment if caught.

Compulsive gamblers who fall into financial ruin will certainly be condemned and punished by family members. Workaholics will also be judged and condemned when family members express their sense of neglect and emotional deprivation. Similar kinds of consequences face husbands and wives who compulsively pursue extra-marital affairs.

Frances, a twenty-eight-year-old former cocaine user who still occasionally used marijuana, frequently found herself acting out being condemned and punished. She was living with a boyfriend who was easily roused to anger and had beat her physically on several occasions. She was five feet tall and weighed 105 pounds, and said in a session after a fight with her boyfriend, "I'm too tiny; he's bigger than me. I can't match him. I can't fight back."

She had fantasies of "smashing back" at him, which was a defense against her attachment to feeling helpless and overwhelmed: "You see, I don't want this feeling of being helpless, I want to smash him." Instead of smashing back, however, she would cower in a corner of their apartment, sobbing and whimpering while her boyfriend stood over her berating her angrily.

Frances had a problem with her boss who, she felt, disliked her and was poised to fire her at any time. "He has this power over me," she protested. "But I can't lose my job. I'm stuck there, I have to pay off a huge credit-card bill."

She also had an excessive fear of being raped and had dreams and fantasies of being alone on a camping trip when accosted by criminals. She became intensely anxious one time when she saw a half-naked child wandering down a street and was furious at her boyfriend for not immediately rushing to the child's "rescue." She had identified with the child and the child's presumed helplessness. Her feelings of helplessness were often accompanied by feelings of being inadequate, less than, not wanted, excluded, worthless. Often she slipped into feelings of being a hopeless case, and in her misery she noted how apathetic and self-pitying she became.

"These feelings pull me down like quicksand," Frances said. "And sometimes I don't even try to pull myself out."

From this emotional state she then fell into what she called "severe helplessness." Years earlier she had contemplated suicide. Once in a session she said in exasperation, "I can't come out of my depression. I can't help my boyfriend cope with his life, and when I try I can't even help my friends deal with their problems."

Such individuals have a compulsion to punish and condemn themselves for their "naughty" behavior, their runaway desires, for being "out of control," for having "no will power," for being "no-good failures," and "worthless bums," and so on. Out of these feelings comes a willingness to be more aligned with dying than with living.

To help the reader understand more about this thesis, it is important to provide academic background. As stated earlier, Freud believed in a self-destructive element in the psyche, which he called the "death drive." In 1930 in *Civilization and Its Discontents* he wrote:

"What methods does culture use to inhibit counteracting aggression, to neutralize the latter, or even to exclude it? . . . This can be studied in the development of the individual . . . The method is very strange, and at the same time very obvious, although we did not guess it. The aggression becomes introjected, internalized; finally it is returned to its place of origin, hence directed against the individual's own ego. There it is absorbed by one particular sector of the ego, the superego, which is counterposed to the other parts of the ego. Now conscience exhibits toward the ego that identical severe readiness to aggression which the ego would have liked to expend on an outside individual. We call this tension between the severe superego and the subjugated ego feeling of guilt; it manifests itself in the need for punishment."

In 1932, Freud again noted the cruelty of the superego (the seat of self-aggression) when he wrote, "The superego seems to have made a one-sided selection, to have chosen only the harshness and severity of the parents, their preventive and punitive function, while their loving care is not taken up and continued by it."

Freud also said in *Civilization and Its Discontents,* "The assumption of the existence of an instinct of death or destruction has met with resistance even in analytic circles . . . To begin with it was only tentatively that I put forward the views I have developed here, but in the course of time they have gained such a hold upon me that I can no longer think in any other way. . . . I remember my own defensive attitude when the idea of an instinct of destruction first emerged in psychoanalytic literature, and how long it took before I became receptive to it. That others should have shown, and still show, the same attitude of rejection surprises me less. For little children do not like it when there is talk of the inborn human inclination to 'badness,' to aggressiveness and destruction, and so to cruelty as well. God has made them in the image of His own perfection; nobody wants to be reminded how hard it is to reconcile the undeniable existence of evil . . . with His all-powerfulness or His all-goodness."

The notion of a death drive may be more acceptable under another name. In 1987 psychiatric authorities introduced the diagnosis "Self-Defeating Personality Disorder" in the edition of the *Diagnostic and Statistical Manual of Mental Disorders,* the primary reference book for all mental-health professionals. The diagnosis is still considered controversial because of the implications of widespread unconscious masochism (which mental-health professionals and ordinary people absolutely hate to acknowledge as a fundamental flaw of our human nature), and the new diagnosis was included in an appendix of the manual under categories needing further study.

A few years before his death, Freud wrote in *Analysis Terminable and Interminable* (1937), "There exists no stronger impression of the resistances during analytic work than that of a force defending itself by every means against recovery and wanting absolutely to cling to illness and suffering. . . Looking over the whole picture, with the added phenomena of immanent (primary) masochism in so many people . . . and the inner guilt of neurotics, one can no longer hold to the belief that psychic life is exclusively ruled by the pursuit of pleasure."

This force described by Freud is, I believe, the biggest obstacle facing addictive personalities. Every day in sessions I see this dark force that defends against recovery and growth. Some individuals in their first session profess a fervent desire to change and then fail to appear for the following session. Others make good progress in therapy and, poised for new insight and growth, suddenly quit their therapy. Sometimes the resistance consists of an inability to tolerate the feeling of having their defenses breached. They claim to want change but are too entangled in their attachments.

Sometimes an addict says, "I know what you're saying

about me is right. But I don't want to face this, I don't want to deal with it." One addict commented: "I'm caught, I'm stuck, I'm too weak to make it, I just can't turn this around."

The problem is not that he cannot do it; the problem is that unconsciously he is not willing to give up his secret attachments. Often codependents fight a losing battle trying to reform addicts, who in turn hate the codependents for trying. That is because the addicts are now refusing good (as well as clinging to their attachments), which makes them feel even more guilty.

Addictive personalities are not alone in resisting positive change. People plagued by low self-esteem and caught in family strife, bad relationships, career failure, fears, and stress also resist making changes for the better.

It seems sometimes that addictive personalities are the flagellants of the twentieth century. In the Middle Ages crowds of flagellants roamed the countryside, whipping themselves and one another, convinced their suffering would atone for the sins of humanity that they believed were the cause of the Black Death and other plagues. Addictive personalities also inflict themselves with unnecessary suffering. They whip themselves with guilt, shame, and condemnation for their substance abuse and other "sins." They cry in chorus, "I am bad. I deserve to be punished. I cause this terrible suffering to happen through my flaws, defects, disease, or sins." The more they focus on their "sins" such as being weak, selfish, or mean, the more they fail to see the underlying attachments. The insights of science provided antidotes for those old plagues of the flesh, and psychological insights into unconscious functioning (not a focus on the "sins" themselves) offer antidotes for addictions and compulsions, modern-day plagues of the spirit.

Let us look again at the nature of secret attachments. How is it that they have such a powerful influence on our behavior? Every child is born with an allotment of natural aggression. This aggression is healthy and appropriate; it is an instinctive survival mechanism. To be successful in life, to prosper and to grow, takes aggression. Aggression is required in order to tell someone, "I love you and I want you." In contrast, aggression that leads to abuse or violence is the negative expression of this quality.

Freud contended that some aggression is turned inward against the child. The child kicks and screams in temper tantrums when expressing his frustration at the affronts to his self-centeredness. But the child is too weak and helpless to vent all his aggression into the environment. This is because of the limitations imposed by the infant's weak musculature. Later, the child feels restrained by social constraints and fears of punishment. The only avenue for remaining aggression is against his own self. (Aggression is a drive; it is dynamic and requires some form of expression.) Thus the child becomes the target of his own aggression and the tendency of all humans to be plagued by self-aggression or the death drive has become operational.

Edmund Bergler took this a step further. He said the self-aggression or the death drive is so powerful because it is sustained by unconscious attachments to the feeling of the aggression acting against the self. As mentioned earlier, the attachments develop when a child in protecting his illusion of omnipotence is convinced emotionally that whatever happens to him, even unpleasant experiences such as being refused and deprived, are products of his own wishes. He succeeds in creating an unconscious affinity for what would otherwise feel like displeasure. This softens the blow of self-aggression but entangles him in its complex web, as if his psyche has become host to a self-defeating parasite.

Displeasure made pleasurable rises into consciousness with sexual masochists. These individuals have libidinized the feeling of being verbally or physically abused; they are conscious of the sexual rush they get from such abuse. Sexual masochists, Bergler believed, represent the tip of a psychic iceberg. He said that everyone has, in degrees, secret attachments that he considered masochistic in nature. An individual usually feels no conscious pleasure from the effect of these attachments—only suffering. But there are exceptions. One client who had been rejected by her boyfriend masturbated for hours in her bedroom, conscious of the degree to which she was sexually aroused by the feeling of having been discarded and abandoned. Her sexual pleasure, however, was soon replaced by depression and feelings of worthlessness.

A major aspect of self-aggression is self-reproach in the form of tormenting inner voices. In addictive personalities especially, inner voices or dialogue feel like broadcasting stations playing at full volume variations of doubt, mocking reproach, and hard-rock condemnation. Alcohol and drugs can serve as an antidote because they can temporarily bolster the ego, thereby temporarily neutralizing or silencing the inner voices (superego). Often addicts overdose on alcohol or drugs because only in becoming comatose can they block out the mocking, scolding, reproachful inner voices.

In extreme cases, these voices intrude to such extent that they take over the personality and establish an unrelenting tyranny of the mind. The person's ego is completely overpowered, and he becomes the embodiment of these inner voices. The babbling of schizophrenics is the vocalization of inner voices. In cases of psychosis or schizophrenia, these voices may be felt to be outside the self, as the voice of the devil or the voice of a scolding, sarcastic God.

All people, especially addictive personalities, are plagued to some degree by self-aggression in the form of these inner voices. Very often the harsh mocking voices are unconscious or subliminal. The voices accuse us of failure, incompetency, selfishness, neglect, wrong-doing, and so on. I have alluded to these voices throughout the book. Initially, they are first unconscious as they accuse the individual of indulging in some secret attachments: "You really are attached to emptiness, being seen as no good, feeling deprived of love, aren't you?" The unconscious ego defends, "No, no, see how I give excitement and good feelings to myself with alcohol and drugs. That means I want to get."

Now the inner voices move on to the next stage of attack. The voices often rise into the individual's consciousness as they begin to torment him for his weaknesses in abusing substances or in being compulsive: "You are a no-good failure. You're not supposed to be using drugs and alcohol. You are a wash-out, and again you have failed. This is the way it is with you. One failure after another. You are bad and deserve to be punished."

Now the individual descends into his personal hell, experiencing the full brunt of his self-aggression. He uses his problems with alcohol, drugs, food, promiscuity, compulsive gambling, and so on as evidence that he is bad and deserves to be the recipient of this self-aggression. Meanwhile, he can cover up his willingness to be the target of his own aggression by believing his addictions or compulsions are the problems in themselves and that they are caused by a "disease" beyond his control, or by chemistry, genes, parents, or society. In doing this, he truly accentuates his victim mentality.

This happened with Tina. As a child, performance was the standard by which she was measured. She had felt that being "a good little girl" and "an excellent student" were prerequisites for her father's and mother's love. Insecurity and lack of self-esteem plagued her college years, and she barely managed to obtain her degree. By twenty-one, she was abusing drugs and alcohol.

Tina had attachments to being seen in a negative light.

She expected to do badly, to be seen as inadequate and not good enough. Her self-defeating behavior with alcohol, drugs, and relationships became an exhibition of her secret attachment to being seen negatively. Meanwhile, she was floundering in feelings of helplessness, shame, and guilt, blaming herself for being no good, a dismal failure.

She adopted the addict's ultimate defense, to embark on "an addiction attack" or orgy of bingeing to draw attention away from the underlying attachments. This defense contends, "I'm not attached to being seen as no good. The problem is, I'm an addict. I'm out of control. I'm impotent. I have no will. I have this disease that just takes over."

As always, in defending against her attachment to being seen as no good, her defense prompted her to act out being seen as no good. At least now she could make her claim to power: "I cause it to happen."

Tina now had to contend with the punishing inner voices that berated her for "causing it to happen." She embarked on a psychological inner beating—guilt, remorse, sense of failure, shame, self-reproach. She rationalized, "Nothing works. I've tried every program and nothing works." She felt sorry for herself, which is always a sign of indulgence in some secret attachment.

Her emotions translated into an unconscious acceptance of condemnation and punishment, hence the addictive personality's cycles of self-denigration and self-torture. She became lost in the maze of her defenses, miles from the roots where her torments began.

Another client was recovering from her bulimia but still had episodes in which she binged on food. Following binges, she had always experienced intense self-condemnation for her behavior with the food. From therapy, she began to recognize the harsh inner voices of condemnation as an impersonal force of self-aggression. In the process of working out her attachments to disapproval and condemnation, she began to refrain from taking the condemning words to heart. As a result, she no longer felt the compulsion to act out being bad or naughty, and the temptations to binge became rare and weak.

Many addictive personalities have more than one addiction and compulsion, suggesting they are predisposed to pursue the feelings of deprival, control, rejection, criticism, and so on through whatever avenues lead there.

A distinction here is important. It is *not* suffering that the addict is seeking. Rather, suffering is the consequence of the addictive personality's secret willingness to indulge in feeling deprivation, control, rejection, condemnation, and so on.

Clients ask, "How can I be attached to such negative experiences? How can this be? How could this have happened to me? It sounds so sick!"

How does the baby account for the painful experience of not having the milk immediately available? Since his first instinct is to preserve the illusion of megalomania, he discovers he can take credit for hurting himself. He begins to feel he must have wanted the unpleasant experiences. How otherwise, given his conviction of omnipotence, could it possibly be happening to him?

He feels, therefore, that what he is doing to himself is what he wants and what he likes. This "solution" makes it possible for him to preserve the cherished megalomania. "It may hurt," the child's consciousness deduces, "but at least I am doing it to myself." Deep within, the child is able to libidinize or "sugar-coat" the feeling of being refused and not getting.

This sugar-coating process is exemplified in the followers of a religious or cult leader. When the leader takes his followers on some journey that produces deprivations and suffering, they ask him, "What is happening? Why are we suffering so much?" The cult leader, whose ego will not accept the disaster of his leadership (as the child will not divest his mock-throne), replies, "This is the way God wants it. This is God's plan for us; we have to suffer because this is the way we are recognized as special." Once the followers believe this, they are able to tolerate the suffering and even take gratification in it. By believing the suffering makes them special, they come to embrace it.

As an example of this, I refer to the hundreds of American followers of Jim Jones who committed suicide in the jungle of Guyana in 1978. These self-defeated people had identified themselves as victims of American society, and they played the victim role to the end, dying in the emotional conviction of their special relationship to God.

Addictive personalities can defeat the tyranny of secret attachments and win inner peace for themselves. Peace comes when the previously self-defeating mechanisms rise into awareness where they are cut to shreds by the individual's intelligence and determination. This is what it means to shape one's life, to become the hero and heroine of one's own destiny, rather than a victim of fate.

Chapter 13

Epilogue

Nothing is more splendid than to rise triumphant from the inner tyranny of secret attachments. Separation from one's secret attachments requires a challenging inner journey. Like Marco Polo setting off for China, you are not quite sure where you are going, what you will find, or whether you will even make it.

It is also something of a "magical mystery tour," this journey to be free of irrational self-defeating forces. Many modern treatments approach emotional distress as a medical problem. But it is first and foremost a problem of unconscious and irrational operations. With insight, we begin to dismantle the negative influence of these operations.

The greatest mystery that we can solve is to fathom the reasons why we fall so easily into negativity and thereby diminish the experience of our lives.

The exploration of the unconscious is a sacred affair. The endeavor reveals aspects of our essence, spirit, or soul. One client struggling for freedom from his chronic emotional distress told me, "I feel I have an illness of the soul." A few days later a woman said in my office, "It feels like my soul hurts."

Much is at stake in each person's recovery and personal growth. For every person who sees into his own inner self, and solves his emotional problems, the culture and the nation are strengthened. Meanwhile, we cannot understand society and ourselves without understanding the fundamentals of unconscious functioning.

Psychology reveals the means for a progression of humanity away from anxieties, fears, hatreds, and self-defeat. We have the science for the improvement of our human nature. But that science is not being applied with enough determination or vision.

For those who are weary of addictions and suffering, the following reference points can help:

1. The first step in any recovery program is the admission that you have a problem. A primary element underlying your denial of a problem are your attachments to feelings of being controlled, rejected, and seen as inadequate or a failure. These attachments cause you to hate to do or to consider what is in your best interest.

A problem for addictive personalities is not only denial of their self-damaging behavior (even that eventually becomes apparent to them) but denial of the underlying emotional states that compel them to behave in a self-damaging manner.

Many of you want to blame your negative emotions and self-defeating actions on others, on the doorstep of society, on genetics, or your upbringing. Blaming is an act of deception, a way to preserve the illusion of your innocence in any wrongdoing.

Ask yourself, "Why is it so hard for me to face the truth of what is happening to me? Why is it so hard for me to be abstinent?"

2. Be aware of the belief that nothing works and no one can help. Feelings of powerlessness permeate the mentality of ad-

dictive personalities, revealed in such statements as, "This problem is too overwhelming," or "I can't see myself ever being happy and healthy." An attachment to feeling powerless can make it seem that taking responsibility for your life is an impossible undertaking.

Many feel that recovery and health are not positive outcomes. If you are helped, you may feel reduced. You feel that to be helped is a capitulation or submission to others. You may try to invalidate helpers because you take their efforts as an indication you are inferior or less than. This effect is more pronounced when you are caught up in being insignificant or helpless.

Or you may feel that if therapy or intervention work, that is further evidence you are wrong and others are right. Many just resent help, and secretly want to stay with what is familiar, even if it is painful.

3. Watch for ambivalence. The addictive personality says he needs control and structure to help him manage his life. He is wanting and expecting other people to tell him what to do and to regulate him. This reinforces his helplessness and passivity. But when controls are applied, he resents others for it. Then he rebels, "How dare they try to tell me what to do!"

Here is what addicts feel: if a helper tells them what to do, he is pushing them; if the helper backs off, then he does not care about them. They swing back and forth between these extremes. They feel they are always up against someone who is not helping them. This puts the significant others in their lives in impossible situations.

The entanglement with substance abuse reflects the passivity he feels with others. As he feels forced to submit to a boss, a spouse, co-workers, relatives, or the requirements of daily living, he is inclined to submit to a substance. (An addict who meekly submits when asked to stay overtime at work comes home late in a sour mood and submits to his vodka.) Addicts can ask themselves what they are feeling forced to submit to, in order to try to see their secret attachment to feeling controlled.

4. Understand the point of view of others. This helps the addictive personality to emerge from his profound self-absorption and to empathize with others. He needs to become aware of how much time and energy he devotes to considering how others are viewing him. He feels the eyes of judgment are constantly upon him.

The addict must see that people are not focused on him. They have their own issues, their own problems, involvements, and pleasures. But the addict will use his self-centeredness to enhance the feeling that others are either impressed by him, ignoring him, or disapproving of him.

The addictive personality can learn to avoid interpreting outer situations as "They are out to get me" or "They don't care about me." He can begin to see how ready he is to feel deprived, controlled, disapproved of, and belittled.

We all have a tendency to project onto others our points of view, and our unwanted and unrecognized negative traits, especially when we are self-absorbed. Addicts especially are quick to project their own negative intentions or "hang-ups" onto others. For instance, many addicts accuse others of addictive behavior: "She's really the one with the problem!" Denial, resentment, protest, and resistance often accompany an addict's attempt to see how he projects his own issues onto others.

5. Watch the inclination to take constructive feedback as criticism, especially when the observations come from spouses or family members. This happens in psychotherapy sessions when the client has a reaction to the analysis, takes it as criticism, and feels discredited or put down. He takes the analysis as a commentary on his deficiencies. But there is no judgment in the analysis; it is clinical, offered as insight to help a person

overcome his problems.

Ideally, someone hearing insight about himself is pleased with the new knowledge and encouraged that it will help him to get better. But an addict attached to feeling criticized allows the analysis to feed that side of himself. He needs to become aware of his predisposition to interpret objective statements or actions according to what he is attached to.

6. Chronic anger, anxiety, withdrawal, and depression are the emotional consequences of entanglements in secret attachments. If a person feels rage for someone's cruel refusal or rejection, rage and attempts at retaliation indicate the depth of his attachments to feeling denied or rejected. Rage brings the individual more distress and intensifies his attachment to being a victim.

A healthy individual victimized by cruelty or injustice may indeed be angry, but he has more ability to deal with it patiently and effectively. He is more likely to win against his enemies because he is patient and plans his moves wisely. The individual reacting to a secret attachment is more easily provoked. He has less ability to wait since his anger, used as a defense, urgently demands satisfaction. He is more likely to be defeated, by others and by himself. Feelings of guilt accompany his anger and further defeat is unconsciously expected.

When you feel angry, try to go beneath the anger to the hidden feelings that have created the anger. Ask yourself, "Why am I so angry? What do I feel they did to me?" Ask yourself when feeling victimized, "Am I dwelling on this event or person or feeling, and extracting every morsel of hurt, and adding this injustice to my collection?"

Stated in its simplest form, the progression goes like this: a) unconsciously you are drawn to hold onto feelings of being deprived, controlled, rejected, etc. and will even scan the environment to look for opportunities to become entangled in these feelings; b) this is covered up by defensive reactions such as righteous indignation, protest, anger, retaliation, withdrawal, depression, anxiety and the excessive need for approval; c) you feel compelled to engage in addictive, compulsive, or other self-defeating behavior as your defenses shift you further away from what is really happening underneath.

7. Take risks. Assert yourself with strength, dignity, and grace when you perceive that someone is unjust or mean to you. A passive client was burdened with the worst jobs in his office. In a calm tone, he finally said to his boss: "This arrangement is not fair. I have most of the unpleasant projects here, as everyone is aware. I would appreciate more sharing of tasks, so that I get some duties that offer more opportunity to develop skills and to be creative."

Making this statement was frightening for him. But he got what he asked for. Even if his request had been denied, he would have felt better simply for asking. Growth and personal development require that we honor ourselves, and that means taking risks. For growth, you must venture beyond the boundaries of your identity, beyond your sense of who you are and what you are able or entitled to do. Even when you take cautious steps in this direction, it can generate anxiety and fear. Remember that fear is often used as an excuse to stay in your passivity.

Do not be afraid to be wrong. Even if you overreact or say the "wrong" thing, you will gain respect for having spoken up, providing you are not belligerent. As you act on your feelings, and understand the significance of your emotions, you will learn to become more appropriate.

8. Watch the tendency to compare yourself to others. When you use situations to compare yourself unfavorably, you are looking for ways to slip into feelings of disapproval. This causes you to feel bad about yourself. If you compare yourself with others and feel that you are superior, you may be

exhibiting arrogance, which itself is a defense against feelings of inferiority.

If you are comparing yourself with others, you may also be fishing around for the feeling of being deprived. You can imagine that others are better off and have more of something than you do. Secret attachments to deprival and the feeling of missing out on something are the driving forces behind "Keeping up with the Joneses." Or you may long to be like someone you believe is more powerful than you, in order to compensate for your attachments to helplessness and passivity.

9. Accept that the world is sometimes unfair. This way you have one less reason to feel victimized. Life will always present you with a steady diet of aggravations and encounters with difficult people. Watch the predisposition to make a tragedy out of a nuisance. Use obstacles and adversity to whet your courage and dignity. It is not your job to straighten out the world but rather to handle your own little world.

Life will not always be comfortable and people can expect disappointments. Misfortunes are not encountered specifically for you to suffer; it is your attachments and narcissism that hold you in the emotional conviction that events are supposed to correspond with your expectations. Watch those expectations. If certain results are realistically beyond reach, then farfetched expectations are a compensation for an attachment to feelings of deprivation or missing out.

Remember that secret attachments reside within yourself. You cannot run away from them. When attachments remain in place, a new wife, a new job, or a new residence provide only temporary distraction and relief from emotional distress. Unresolved emotional issues will continue to be transferred onto new people and new settings. When you work out your secret attachments, life will not seem so unfair. Pleasure will be found where it was missing before.

10. Work through your emotional reactions. This requires the addictive personality to define with sufficient insight how he feels about a problem that has come up, to determine the negative feeling he is holding onto, and to take personal responsibility for the feeling. Some people do not get far with this: the tendency is so strong to focus on what others are doing to them rather than to understand their own reactions.

For many people, help from a psychotherapist is necessary to penetrate their defenses and to gain insight into emotional reactions. Keep a journal and note your daily reactions to others and life's events. This will help you to identify patterns and recurring feelings.

During the working-through phase, it is important to acknowledge emotionally your resistance to letting go of gripes and wounds. The addictive personality needs to feel how, emotionally, he is attached to feeling opposed, disliked, oppressed. He needs to understand and feel his secret wish to maintain his negative attachments in spite of his conscious desires and statements to the contrary. There is great resistance here: recognition on an emotional level of your secret attachments offends your narcissism and tastes like bitter medicine.

The addictive personality may become aware of a sense of mourning and sadness for what he feels he has missed out on in his life, for what he did not get in his childhood. This "crying over spilled milk" puts his life on hold. The result is a shying away from intimacy, from receiving and getting, from love, thus repeating the cycle which began in childhood.

11. Watch the tendency to be critical of yourself for "not doing well enough." Recovery and growth take time. Addicts are up against a powerful "enemy within" that is able to take possession of their personality. It takes time for you to see and understand the operations involved in liberating yourself. Beating up on yourself for every little misdemeanor makes it worse.

Metaphorically, self-reproach is a little demon sitting on your shoulder. He is whispering,"You're kidding yourself, you are going nowhere, Bub. You're a loser and you know it!" Or he might say, "Look at you, you screwed up again! You were supposed to quit that bad behavior and you didn't! You're a lost cause!" Your tendency is to "buy into" the little demon's nasty accusations. This inner voice is an unconscious drive, an alien energy that constitutes your self-aggression in action. Recognizing your malevolent inner voice as self-aggression makes it is easier to refrain from taking its message or "put-downs" seriously.

When an addict is upset about progressing too slowly, he may be indulging in feeling that he is missing out on the benefits of full recovery. This is just another way to feel deprived. If he is on the right path, time is on his side.

Growth does not have to be hard work. A person can play with his new awareness, see it as an intriguing process of discovery. Difficult experiences or situations are used as learning opportunities rather than hardships to be endured. As a person sees more deeply into events, he develops his capacity to make better decisions. He understands that it is not always a matter of what he does–but rather how he feels about what he does. A person can make a correct decision (i.e. leaving the children with a baby-sitter) and yet feel guilty about it (perhaps because he imagines the children are feeling unloved or abandoned as he identifies with them).

12. Recreate positive life scenarios. An addict can begin to see himself as strong and steady. At first, this vision of himself may be only a glimmer, a minor star light-years away. But aligned with recovery and growth, and holding onto his vision, his star becomes brighter.

Following a period of abstinence and working through of self-defeating attachments, the clouds of confusion, aloneness, and dejection dissipate. The individual sees clearly that he is in charge of his life, and that he has more choices in how to live and express himself. Without trying to force it, he begins to create positive life scenarios. He goes after what he says he wants and makes those changes he has been wanting to make.

He chooses a healthier lifestyle and healthier friends. The issues that formerly produced misery or suffering wither away and die. An individual no longer feels a frantic need to be recognized and praised. Happiness no longer rests on outside judgment. Words and actions are no longer split (say one thing but do another). He is integrated; his life reflects the transformation he has achieved.

Many individuals, and especially addictive personalities, have difficulty discovering meaning or purpose for their lives because they are so caught up surviving each day's emotional rigors. Without purpose, an individual is adrift, prey to the fates, hungry and lonely, hearing the siren call of misadventure.

Purpose is more than career prospects. A sincere effort to recover from addictions and compulsions brings a great sense of higher purpose to one's life. One can sense the struggle for recovery and insight as an epic journey, a heroic struggle that gives his life meaning. Purpose involves caring for loved ones, for community, the environment, the next generation, and in enriching the capacity for wonder and joy.

Once emotional hooks are gone, and individuals no longer look for offense or feel dissatisfied with what they have, compassion is born. Compassion makes no demands that anything or anyone be different from what is. Compassion does not mean one feels the need to help someone. It is a soft and stirring pleasure in the heart of one freed from self-absorption.

Compassion feels life's experiences intensely and allows one to observe others and external events in a state of serenity and peacefulness. Compassion is not necessarily "for this" or "against that." It inspires a person to bring forth what is best in himself, as paradoxically it accepts the negative and the positive, accepts an absence of peace and a lack of control over events.

Along with wisdom, peace and purpose, compassion is one of the great prizes bestowed on those who overthrow the tyranny of secret attachments.

Bibliography

Bergler, Edmund. *Curable and Incurable Neurotics.* Liveright, New York, 1961.

Bergler, Edmund. *Principles of Self-Damage.* The Philosophical Library, 1958.

Bergler, Edmund. *The Superego.* Grune and Stratton, New York, 1952.

Elkind, David. *Child Development and Education: A Piagetian Perspective.* Oxford University Press, New York, 1976.

Diagnostic And Statistical Manual of Mental Disorders (Third Edition–Revised). American Psychiatric Association, Washington, D.C. 1987.

Gay, Peter. *Freud: A Life For Our Time.* W.W. Norton & Co., New York, 1990.

Gay, Peter. *The Freud Reader.* W.W. Norton & Co., New York, 1989.

LeShan, Lawrence. *The Dilemma of Psychology.* Dutton, New York, 1990.

Klein, Melanie, *The Psychology of Children.* London, 1934.

Miller, Alice, *For Your Own Good.* Farrar, Straus, Giroux, New York, 1983.

Peele, Stanton. *Diseasing of America: Addiction Treatment Out of Control.* Lexington Books. Lexington, MA 1989.

Richmond, P.G., *An Introduction to Piaget.* Basic Books Inc., New York, 1971.

Selected Papers of Edmund Bergler, M.D. (1933-1961). Grune and Stratton, New York, 1969.

About the Author

Peter Michaelson is a psychotherapist in private practice and a graduate of Antioch University with a Master of Arts degree in psychology and counseling. Before becoming a psychotherapist, he worked for fifteen years as a professional journalist and specialized in reporting on science and health topics. Mr. Michaelson gives seminars on self-esteem and the emotional problems of addictive personalities. For several years he has been training other psychotherapists in his clinical methods.

Excerpt from *See Your Way To Self-Esteem:*

Celebrity Peeping

Whenever the average person spots a celebrity in the flesh, he has an emotional reaction that usually varies according to his self-esteem and also the degree to which the celebrity is famous.

If the celebrity you see is the local TV weatherman, your eyes might soak him or her up for an instant or two, and then you will go about your business with a minimum of emotional disruption.

However, if the celebrity is a high-flying Hollywood movie star, your eyes fasten like rivets to his or her body and, depending on your self-esteem, you could be instantly transported into an altered consciousness complete with rapid pulse and sweaty palms.

The lower your own self-esteem, the greater will be your emotional thrill in being in the presence of a celebrity. The cult of the celebrity is a cultural anomaly that flourishes under the auspices of the low self-esteem of the masses. Your self-esteem is also inversely proportional to the time you spend fantasizing about being a celebrity.

Within the cult of celebrity, fame matters more than substance. A celebrity's validation by the culture, not our own personal judgment of his worth, determines his status in our eyes. If Benedict Arnold returned to modern America in a blaze of media attention, it is probable that millions of people would want to shake his hand and stand bedazzled in his presence. It is not the possibility of reincarnation that would be exciting them but the emotional thrill of feeling their own selves being observed, noticed, and perhaps even acknowledged by someone deemed a VIP.

Since the typical person feels his own value only to a relative degree, he relishes any emotional surges of good feelings about himself. A celebrity's notice of him (or the prospect that a celebrity will at any moment notice him) makes the average person feel that he counts for something other than his everyday anonymity. One of my clients said his main claim to fame was a three-day drunk he passed with a famous stuntman.

Just about everyone has shortcomings of self-esteem. Even successful and prominent people at times inwardly reproach themselves for alleged failures, inadequacy, even worthlessness, while entangled in their psyches' fears and dissatisfactions. How many times has a movie star's inner conscience tormented him for not being more famous? Under that accusation, this movie star would feel grateful for the fans cheering him as he walked into the opening night showing of his latest big hit. "You see," his defenses could say to his mocking inner conscience or super-ego, "you're wrong–I am somebody important. Look how many people recognize my value."

Just about everyone is under some degree of accusation from his inner conscience to the effect that he is unimportant and insignificant. A person with low self-esteem is often bullied by his inner conscience, "You won't amount to anything! You're always screwing up! You're a loser! And everybody knows it!"

To compensate, it is convenient to identify with celebrities, to imagine what it would be like to be in the shoes of one VIP or another. This can provide a satisfactory defense for our attachments to feeling inadequate and worthless. "This is how I would like to be!" proclaims the inner defense. "This is how I would like to feel! This is what I want for myself!"

Put another way, most of us labor under the feeling of not being recognized for who we are and what we do. So when we stand in the presence of a celebrity, we not only rub shoulders with him, we rub psyches, eager to pick up some of the magical omnipotence of someone whose self-importance is exposed for all neurotics to see and admire. "You see, this is what I really would like," we plea in our unconscious defense." I'm tired feeling like a worthless, unknown nobody."

I saw my first celebrity at age fourteen. Not a lot of them showed up in the north woods where I lived, but one day I walked into our jukebox hangout and saw Little Beaver, a midget wrestler, sitting on a stool sipping a milkshake. I scampered across the street, plunked down my chocolate sundae money for a pen and pad, and hurried back for his autograph. It may have been the only one he gave out that day, but he got me high without my sugar boost.

In psychoanalytic language, celebrities are personifications of our ego-ideal. The ego-ideal is the grandiose version of ourselves formed in childhood when our megalomania or extreme self-centeredness is most pronounced. Naive childhood beliefs—such as "I'll be president (or great at something) when I grow up"—illustrate the essence of this idealized self.

So we project our own idealized self onto celebrities. They are what we would like to be. We see in them our idealized self. Later in life, our inner conscience is always ready to torture us with criticism and reproach when our lives do not measure up to the expectations of our idealized self. When we "buy into" the negative messages of that impersonal, even alien, side of ourselves, we believe the worst about ourselves and feel like lonely nobodies. Then celebrities seem to us like gods. ❧